John C. Howell, a nationally respected trial lawyer, was admitted to the Florida Bar in 1955 and to the Colorado Bar in 1970. He has also been admitted to practice before all federal and state courts in those states, including the United States Supreme Court. A graduate of the University of Miami Law School, Mr. Howell has practiced extensively in corporate law. He is now a member or former member of the American Bar Association, the Federation of Insurance Counsel, the Legal Research Institute, and the American Arbitration Association. Author of a number of law review articles, Mr. Howell has also published sixteen books to date.

THE COMPLETE CITIZEN'S LAW LIBRARY
_____

The Complete Guide to Business Contracts

Corporate Executive's Legal Handbook

Estate Planning for the Small Business Owner

Form Your Own Corporation

Prepare Your Own Partnership Agreements

John C. Howell

ESTATE PLANNING FOR THE SMALL BUSINESS OWNER

Avoid personal liability, legal fees, and unnecessary expenses

A SPECTRUM BOOK

Prentice-Hall, Inc., Englewood Cliffs, New Jersey 07632

Library of Congress Cataloging in Publication Data

HOWELL, JOHN COTTON, 1926-
Estate planning for the small business owner.

(A Spectrum Book)
Edition for 1979 published under title: Compre-
hensive estate planning for the small business owner.
1. Estate planning—United States.   2. Inheritance
and transfer tax—United States.   3. Small business—
Taxation—United States.   I. Title.
KF750.H65   1980   346.7305'2   80-15426
ISBN 0-13-289637-0 (pbk.)

For the purposes of editorial simplification, this publication generally uses the
masculine pronoun in the generic sense, to indicate *person*. The author and the
publisher are fully aware that the information in this volume pertains to
women as well as men, and no discrimination is implied or intended.

PRENTICE-HALL INTERNATIONAL, INC., *London*
PRENTICE-HALL OF AUSTRALIA PTY. LIMITED, *Sydney*
PRENTICE-HALL OF CANADA, LTD., *Toronto*
PRENTICE-HALL OF INDIA PRIVATE LIMITED, *New Delhi*
PRENTICE-HALL OF JAPAN, INC., *Tokyo*
PRENTICE-HALL OF SOUTHEAST ASIA PTE. LTD., *Singapore*
WHITEHALL BOOKS LIMITED, *Wellington, New Zealand*

Contents

vi

Preface

Since the enactment of the new tax laws in 1976, over 97 percent of American citizens are exempted from federal estate taxes. The other 2 percent to 3 percent who have estates in excess of the exemptions can generally afford to pay estate planning experts for professional assistance. Even if you have—or expect to have—an estate in excess of the exempt amounts, you can still save a lot of legal fees by learning the estate planning facts in this book instead of paying $50 to $100 per hour to have a lawyer explain them to you.

If you want to do it yourself, take comfort in knowing that several years ago an assembly sponsored by the American Bar Association reported that "The development of procedures for transferring property without administration should be encouraged, as should do-it-yourself techniques" (*American Bar Association Journal,* January 1977, page 88).

Gathering information and ideas for the research and writing of this book has been spread out over 25 years of an enjoyable and rewarding law practice. The dramatic changes in the new tax code and my recent semiretirement from active full-time law practice to write the Citizens Law Library set the stage for the publication of this book at this time. This is, indeed, a most favorable time for this publication because, among other things:

1. Attorneys fees are simply too high for most folks;
2. There has been a great need for an estate planning book for laymen for a long, long time;
3. Most readers can do a very good job in handling their own estate planning with the aid of this book;
4. If your assets do not exceed the new exempt amounts you can write your own will without incurring serious estate tax problems; and
5. You need to know all about the facts, information and ideas in this book regardless of whether you decide to do your own estate planning or employ an attorney.

You can use the information in this book to write your own will, execute the will in accordance with the requirements of your state statutes while saving a lot of time, money, worry, and frustration. I know there may be the unusual or extraordinary case which requires professional help, but this does not detract from the plain fact that most citizens can write their own wills and do their own estate planning. This book is all you will need. For those few who need professional help, this book will guide you in the right direction. You will know what questions to ask, whether the answers make sense, and how to avoid intimidation and overpayment of fees.

Almost all books about estate planning and wills are written by experts for attorneys or other professionals. Few books have ever been written for laymen on this subject. Those that have been written for the layman almost always advise in vague, general terms that in order to finally determine the answers to most questions the reader must check the statutes of his own state or consult an expert. This is the first book ever published that contains a summary of the statutes governing wills for all 50 states and the District of Columbia. With the information contained in Chapter 7 you will know precisely what your state statute provides—and all other states in which you are interested.

Many attorneys who are in the general practice of law will find this book extremely helpful because of the summary of all state statutes on wills. In fact, the material in this book is taken, in large part, from my law office manual which I used for many years writing wills for clients who had no special tax problems. It will be a handy reference for any law office and will be of great value to anyone who has an interest in estate planning and will writing.

The summary of state statutes reflects the statutes available in 1980. Although these statutes do not change significantly or very often, you should always be alert to revisions in your statutes. You should be especially inter-

ested in the possibility of your state adopting the Uniform
Probate Code.

ESTATE PLANNING FOR THE SMALL BUSINESS OWNER

1

What Is Estate Planning?

The term *estate planning* has undergone an expanding series of definitions during the past few years. It means different things to different people. To the professional estate planner or to a lawyer who specializes in estate planning it means one thing and to you and me it may have a different meaning. It has a different purpose and meaning to a person who is 21 years of age than it does to a person who is 91.

Estate planning has been defined as the process of planning the accumulation, conservation, and distribution of an estate. Estate planning is the creation, conservation, and utilization of family resources to obtain the maximum support and security for the family during the lifetime and after the death of the planner. Controlled estate planning is a systematic process for uncovering problems and providing solutions in the areas of excessive taxes and transfer costs, lack of liquidity, improper disposition of assets, inadequate income at retirement, inadequate income if disabled, inadequate income for your family after your death, insufficient capital, and other problems.

1

A time honored concept is that estate planning begins with the establishment of four elements:

1. A home, a place to live;
2. An income, usually secured by a job, profession, or business;
3. A savings account, a reserve fund which can be drawn on in case of emergency; and
4. Life insurance, a source of future income if the planner should die.

Classically, most books, seminars, lectures, and other discussions of estate planning by lawyers and other professional estate planners are based upon the old, outdated, traditional notion that the man of the family is the person who earns a living for the other family members; that the wife and children are semihelpless in the area of earning money, managing money, or supporting themselves; and that the primary focus of estate planning is for the husband to plan his affairs so as to take the responsibility for all immediate family members and all descendants (collateral as well as direct) and to pay a significant percentage of the estate to a battery of lawyers, tax experts, and trust departments of the leading banks. Typically this example of persons for whom estate planning is done has unlimited wealth. This attitude among estate planners evolved from the old English land barons and the so-called industrial "giants" in this country during the last century. This idea and concept, still flourishing in many law offices and bank trust departments, has been obsolete for many years and is completely unrealistic in our modern society. Less than 1 percent of the entire population would fit this category.

First, the tax structure in this country is such that very few people—or taxpaying entities—can assemble and hold large estates. The economic climate is such that a large estate, if assembled, cannot be maintained for extended periods of time.

Second, our modern society no longer has the traditional male "head of the household" family structure. The modern wife and mother is now a worker along with her male counterpart. Many families now have a woman as the sole breadwinner. Many have only a male; most of the others have both a man and woman as employed breadwinners. Moreover, the modern woman whose husband, if any, predeceases her before the adulthood of the children, if any, usually remarries—or goes to work— soon after.

Under these circumstances it is no longer appropriate for estate planning to assume the classic attitude about the home life of American citizens. Specifically, the traditional rule was to plan an estate on the assumption that:

1. The husband was the sole money earner;
2. The husband would predecease the wife;
3. The wife will be helpless and own no assets;

4. All children and grandchildren are minors, incompetents, or otherwise will be dependent upon the decedent;

5. The spouses of the children and grandchildren will be dependent on the decedent;

6. The widow would be absolutely incapable of handling money or managing property;

7. Only a lawyer or trust department of a bank could manage the estate;

8. The widow would be incapable of planning her estate, and thus, the husband must create trusts and trustees to protect her from her own incompetence; and

9. Other unrealistic, old fashioned ideas and concepts.

In our modern society more than 98 percent of the adult population would not fit into this old fashioned notion of estate planning. Therefore, there is no longer a need to plan estates on such grandiose scales. The new concept in estate planning is to realistically view the typical family situation as it is; to face the fact that economic, social, and legal forces have drastically changed the way people live; and to take these into account in making long range estate plans.

Estate planning, for our purposes, should consist of:

1. Your conscious, active, and positive effort to evaluate and analyze your current assets;

2. Your taking steps to earn, save, and retain more in the future;

3. Your effectively using, spending, and investing what is available; and
4. Your making specific, but flexible, plans for transferring those assets during lifetime and after.

It is simply a plan for building your estate; accumulating and holding more capital; increasing the value of all your assets, keeping it, using it, giving it away; and making it available to your dependents, friends, charitable institutions, and the government (by paying taxes of all kinds); and making an intelligent, economical transfer after you are finished with it.

Your estate planning should include your preparation, in writing, of all available information about you, your assets, income, and income producing abilities and potential; an analysis of all current assets, the potential for future accumulation of assets; and an intelligent, pre-planned program for conserving, increasing and using it during your life. It should be reviewed periodically—at least once each year and after any significant changes in your family or financial situation. You should have specific alternative plans in the event death should intervene at any stage.

During your planning process you should consider the following:

1. How your income and assets may be shifted to reduce future liabilities;
2. Accumulate sufficient liquid assets to cover all future

liabilities;

3. Make plans for accumulation of sufficient capital so that investment income will adequately meet family needs in all circumstances;

4. Prepare a plan by which capital may be used in an orderly manner in the event it should be necessary in the future to supplement income; and

5. Crystallize your thinking, discuss your plans with adult members of your family, your named executor, and any business partners or associates so that there should never be a crash and burn situation.

Finally, you should not be emotional, get spooked, or think estate planning means death. In fact, if you have a good plan your longevity may be enhanced. And you don't have to pay a big fee to a battery of lawyers, trust officers, and professional estate planners.

Most estate planning discussions, of necessity, revolve around your government and potential taxes. You owe it to yourself and to your family to plan in such a way that money doesn't needlessly go to the government when you could avoid it with proper planning. Avoiding unnecessary expenses, costs, fees, delays, and frustration of the probate system can also be achieved with good planning.

The Tax Reform Act of 1976 and the Revenue Act of 1978 have revolutionized estate planning for most Americans which has always centered around the significant and ever present tax problems presented to the professional estate planners, or tax experts. The new changes in the tax code raised the exemptions on estate and gift taxes so that most Americans are now totally exempted from them. In fact, reliable estimates are that over 97 percent of the American citizens will be exempted from federal estate taxes because of the higher exemptions. But you still need to plan for it, and in all events you should be familiar with all current laws on taxation. Specific sections of the laws will be discussed later.

2

Preliminary Steps in
Effective Estate Planning

There are several things you should do to prepare for your estate planning. These steps will give you a good idea of what you presently have in your estate; what you wish to obtain by way of accumulating capital; and how you can utilize it effectively to fulfill your duties and responsibilities to yourself and to your family. Here is a list of things you should do to get your estate planning on the right track.

1. *Make An Inventory of All Your Assets.* Prepare a complete inventory of your assets and current income. List all your assets, date of acquisition, the costs, and estimated current values. At this stage list all assets irrespective of whether they would be considered a part of your taxable estate. You should also have a list of the assets of all members of your family. This will give you an objective picture of the relative needs of each member. This inventory will not only help you plan for the future, but it will give you a good view of your past planning and how well you have accomplished your objectives. You

can reach your goals and objectives much easier if you have a clear picture of where you have been, where you are now, and where you wish to go. You will be able to determine, at any particular time, whether you need to revise your plans to accommodate tax changes, changes in your family situation or otherwise. Writing it down on paper helps you crystallize your thinking about how you can achieve your goals and objectives. It is important to have an accurate inventory, and it is equally important for you to keep it current.

2. *Classify Your Assets.* It is recommended that you classify your assets in three categories: (1) cash, (2) assets that can be converted into cash, and (3) assets that will remain as capital. The amount of cash that can be raised with each asset and the problem of converting assets into cash should be analyzed and discussed with adult members of your family and your executor. The tax costs which may result on liquidation of assets should be considered. Your analysis of your assets and how they may be utilized in various contingencies is a very significant family transaction and you should help the other members of your family discuss it objectively and intelligently.

3. *Ascertain Your Debts and Liabilities.* An estimate of the amount of debts and claims that will evolve in the estate should be made. This estimate should include current income tax liabilities, debts, estimate of funeral and last illness expenses, and administration costs. As you

review these items of cost, you should consider all methods to eliminate many of the "probate costs."

4. *Estimated Tax Liability, If Any.* After determining your estimated total value of the assets and deducting the estimated debts, claims, and expenses, you can determine the estate tax liability, if any. One of the principle reasons for having good estate plans is to avoid estate taxes. Even though the new tax laws grant higher exemptions, and most Americans will be exempt, you still need to plan in advance. If your taxable estate exceeds the amount of the exemptions you should plan accordingly.

5. *Liquidation of Liabilities.* Make a schedule for the liquidation of estate liabilities. This exercise should include your spouse and executor. Apply cash amounts from the list of cash assets and assets convertible into cash against the schedules of debts, claims, administration costs, and estate tax liabilities, if any. Compute the income tax cost on the liquidation of the assets. Then see whether there is enough cash left to meet the cash needs of the family during the administration of the estate. This comparison of cash available to the estate will indicate whether it may be necessary for a conversion of other assets to handle the estate costs, or whether additional life insurance may be appropriate.

6. *Advisability of Assignments, Trusts, or Other Probate Avoidance Procedures.* If you determine that you will have a taxable estate you should consider the assign-

11

ment of the remaining assets, or a part of them, to individuals or trusts, or take other measures to reduce the amount of the taxable estate if it is compatible with your overall plans. Essentially you should make your choice as to whether the potential tax liabilities are sufficient to motivate you to make an irrevocable transfer or some other method to avoid taxes and avoid probate. If you have a potential taxable estate you may wish to get professional advice. However, you should not permit tax considerations to dominate your estate planning to the detriment of other objectives.

7. *List of Beneficiaries and Assets of Each.* Prepare a schedule showing the assets that will be in the hands of each beneficiary after distribution. This list should also include the separately owned property of each beneficiary. The annual income available from these sources should be compared with the amount of annual income which you think should be available for each beneficiary. The inheritance taxes, if any, of your state should be considered in evaluating the interests of each beneficiary.

8. *Methods For Reducing Liabilities.* Consider other methods of reducing liabilities. For example, lifetime gifts can still reduce estate tax liability by removing future appreciation in value from your estate. These can also increase assets and income available to members of your family. Here again, you may wish to get professional advice if you have serious tax problems.

9. *Spread Income Tax Liabilities.* Consider the transfer of income producing properties to other members of your family, or to a family corporation or partnership, to save income taxes as well as state taxes.

10. *Retirement.* Make long range plans for your own retirement.

11. *Periodic Review of Estate Plans.* Make certain that you schedule periodic reviews of your estate plans after you have completed them.

12. *Avoid Probate.* You should give serious thought to avoiding the hazards of the probate system. Consider the advisability of obtaining a copy of *How to Use or Avoid Probate,* one of the books in the Citizens Law Library, and sharing it with your executor and family.

Estate Planning File and Inventory of Assets

The importance of keeping good records in estate planning cannot be overemphasized. It is vital. Moreover, good records kept up to date on a permanent basis can significantly reduce the costs and delays in the administration of estates. The following form is your personal file for your estate planning.

PERSONAL ESTATE PLANNING FILE AND RECORD BOOK OF _____

A. Information and Records About Yourself
   1. Full Legal Name:
   2. Home Address:

   3. Phone:
   4. Business Address:

   5. Business Phone:
   6. Date of Birth:
   7. Place of Birth:
   8. Nicknames:
   9. Location of birth certificate:
   10. Location of marriage certificate:
   11. Location of prenuptial agreements, if any:
   12. Social Security No.:

B. Information About Your Spouse, (if any)
   1. Full Legal Name:
   2. Home Address:

   3. Phone:
   4. Business Address:

   5. Business Phone:

6. Date of Birth:

7. Place of Birth:

8. Nicknames:

9. Social Security Number:

C. Children

    1. Children, including adopted children with full legal names, addresses, birth dates, and phone numbers:

    2. Children by previous marriage:

D. Current Dependents, including legal names and relationships, addresses, and phone numbers:

E. Miscellaneous Personal Information

    1. Church:

    2. Military service branch and dates:

    3. Location of discharge papers:

    4. Location of safety deposit box:

    5. Location of health and medical records:

    6. Location of records for donating body or anatomical parts after death:

    7. Location of records of burial plot:

    8. Burial Instructions:

F. Names and Addresses of Advisors

    1. Doctors:

2. Attorney:

3. Accountant:

4. Trust officer:

5. Insurance Agent:

6. Pastor:

7. Broker:

8. Financial counselor:

G. Business and Professional Information

   1. Name and location of current business or profession:

   2. Type of business or profession:

   3. Location of employment contracts and agreements:

   4. Names and addresses of business partners and associates:

   5. Silent partners or other business affiliations:

H. Financial Holdings: List all pertinent information such as names of institutions and account numbers, date of acquisition, price of acquisition, location of certificates, titles, contracts or the like; and whether the holdings are in community property or joint tenancy and with whom, or sole and separate property.

   1. Checking accounts:

   2. Savings accounts:

   3. Credit union accounts:

4. Certificates of deposit and/or other monetary investments:
5. Mortgages, notes, etc.:
6. Common stock:
7. Preferred stock:
8. Bonds:
9. Mutual funds:
10. Real estate and realty:
11. Employment benefits and plans:
12. Trusts, patents, copyrights and other rights of value.

I. Insurance and Annuities: List name of company, date acquired, face amount, type of insurance or annuity, name and address of beneficiary, and other pertinent data.
1. Life insurance owned on own life:
2. Annuities owned on own life:
3. Life insurance owned on life of another:
4. Annuities owned on life of another:
5. Other insurance such as household, automobile, health and accident, and special types. Show data appropriate to each, such as policy number, amount, tenure of coverage.

J. Other Valuable Property: List with status of how title is held.

1. Automobiles, trucks, and other such equipment; include make, model, year, etc.:
2. Boats:
3. Aircraft:
4. Antiques:
5. Jewelry:
6. Art works:
7. Rare books:
8. Coin collections, stamp collections, or other similar valuables:
9. Others:

K. Debts, including name and address of creditors, pertinent information, such as amount of original debt, amount still due, terms of obligation, rate of interest, etc.:
1. Banks:
2. Other loans:
3. Mortgages:
4. Promissory notes:
5. Land contracts:
6. Life insurance loans:
7. Other obligations:

L. Other Information of an Estate Nature
1. Location of last will:
2. Date of latest will:
3. Other:

3

The Unified Estate and Gift Tax Schedule

Before the enactment of the Tax Reform Act of 1976 and the Revenue Act of 1978, the basic estate tax exemption was $60,000. The gift tax exemption was $30,000 plus the annual $3,000 per donee exclusion. The new code introduced a single unified estate and gift tax rate schedule with progressive rates based on cumulative transfers during lifetime and at death. The amount of the estate tax is determined under the new law by applying the unified rates to the cumulative lifetime and deathtime transfers and then subtracting the taxes payable on the lifetime transfers. Since the estate tax bracket depends on cumulative lifetime and deathtime transfers, the result is that taxpayers who transfer their property during life and those who keep their property until death are treated substantially the same way for transfer tax purposes.

Before 1977 gifts made within three years of death were included in the gross estate unless the estate could prove they were not made in contemplation of death. Determination of the fact issue as to the decedent's motives and intentions resulted in a great deal of litigation.

Under the new laws, all transfers made within three years of death are includable in the gross estate regardless of the decedent's motives.

The "unified credit" schedule was phased in over a five year period. After 1980 the unified credit will be $47,000 which is an equivalent exemption of $175,625 in each estate. Beginning in 1981 the exemption will be $175,625 each year thereafter; therefore we will use this amount as the basic exemption in our discussions. This increase in the exemption amounts results in more than 98 percent of the estates being completely exempted from federal estate taxes.

The table on page 21 indicates the estate and gift tax where the transfers occurred after December 31, 1976.

Marital Deduction

The new tax code substantially increases the marital deductions. However it is still limited to one-half of the adjusted gross estate where the amounts are over $500,000. The adjusted gross estate is the gross estate less authorized deductions for such items as expenses, debts, taxes, casualty losses, charitable and marital transfers, and certain transfers to orphans. The maximum estate tax marital deduction is $250,000 or 50 percent of the adjusted gross estate whichever is greater. The $250,000 deduction may be taken irrespective of the 50 percent limitation. The deduction, of course, is limited to the value of any amount

ESTATE AND GIFT TAX TABLE

A Taxable transfer more than—	B But not more than—	C Tax on account in Col A—	D Rate of tax on excess of amount in Col A—
$ 0	10,000	—	18%
10,000	20,000	1,800	20%
20,000	40,000	3,800	22%
40,000	60,000	8,200	24%
60,000	80,000	13,000	26%
80,000	100,000	18,200	28%
100,000	150,000	23,800	30%
150,000	250,000	38,800	32%
250,000	500,000	70,800	34%
500,000	750,000	155,800	37%
750,000	1,000,000	248,300	39%
1,000,000	1,250,000	345,800	41%
1,250,000	1,500,000	448,300	43%
1,500,000	2,000,000	555,800	45%
2,000,000	2,500,000	780,800	49%
2,500,000	3,000,000	1,025,800	53%
3,000,000	3,500,000	1,290,800	57%
3,500,000	4,000,000	1,575,800	61%
4,000,000	4,500,000	1,880,800	65%
4,500,000	5,000,000	2,205,800	69%
5,000,000	—	2,550,800	70%

(See Section 2001(c), Internal Revenue Code.)

which is passing or has passed from the decedent to the surviving spouse. The marital deduction applies to gifts to a spouse during lifetime as well as to dispositions at death.

The new marital deduction provision is as follows:

(A) In general. The aggregate amount of the deductions allowed under this section (computed without regard to this subsection) shall not exceed the greater of
  (i) $250,000, or
  (ii) 50 percent of the value of the adjusted gross estate (as defined in paragraph [2]). IRC 2056 (c) (1)

By way of example: Suppose a decedent left an adjusted gross estate of $300,000. Under the old law the marital deduction would have been limited to $150,000 (50 percent of $300,000). But under the new code $250,000 can be taken.

The new code also provides for an unlimited gift tax marital deduction for the first $100,000 in lifetime gifts to a spouse. Gifts over $100,000 up to $200,000 to a spouse are fully taxed and a 50 percent marital deduction is allowed for gifts over $200,000. Under these new tax measures it is possible for a married person to transfer up to $525,625 without any estate or gift taxes being imposed. For example, a person with an estate of $525,625 could make a lifetime gift of $100,000 to the spouse (fully exempt) and leave the balance of $425,625 (or at least $250,000) to the surviving spouse. The $100,000 gift during lifetime is exempt. The $250,000 exemption would apply to the property left to the surviving spouse leaving the balance of $175,625, the amount of the basic exemption.

Farm and Family Owned Businesses

The Congress finally recognized the inequity and hardship caused by the old laws, especially as applied to farmers and family owned businesses. The new tax code gives substantial benefits and reductions in estate taxes to these farms and other closely held businesses. The new code allows an executor to elect to value real property used for farming or in a closely held business, based on its current value as a farm or in a closely held business, rather than on the basis of its potential "highest and best" use for other purposes, as under the old code. The "special use" valuation cannot reduce the gross estate by more than $500,000. Methods for valuing qualified property are provided, and there are various rules and limitations on the application of this section.

Because of the higher exemptions for gift and estate taxes under the new code many more people will be able to plan estates and write wills without any significant tax problems. It is to your advantage to know these new laws and learn how to take advantage of them. Some of the states impose estate taxes but they are similar to the federal code as to exemptions and exclusions. In the event you have a federal estate tax problem you should also consider your local state tax situation.

State Death Taxes

State death taxes can be broken down into three categories, (1) inheritance tax, (2) estate tax, and (3) additional estate tax to absorb the maximum credit for state death taxes allowable under the federal estate tax law.

1. *Inheritance Tax*. An estate tax, like the federal tax, is imposed on an estate before the distribution. It is levied on the right of the decedent to transfer property at death. An inheritance tax, on the other hand, is levied on the right of the beneficiaries to receive property from the deceased. The tax is measured by the share of the estate passing to each beneficiary.

Beneficiaries are divided into classes: (1) those closely related to the decedent, (2) those related to another degree, and (3) those unrelated. Different exemptions usually are established for each class of beneficiary. The same can be said of the tax rates which apply for each class of beneficiary. Generally a lower inheritance tax results when property passes to a close relative than when the same amount of property passes to a more distant relative or a nonrelative.

2. *Estate Tax*. Only a few states impose estate taxes which are similar in principle to the federal estate tax. In most of these cases, a flat exemption is given to the estate. A few of these states, however, group the beneficiaries in classes and allow an exemption for each beneficiary before imposing a single tax rate on the entire remaining estate.

3. *Additional Estate Tax*. Most states have the provi-

sion that if their inheritance and/or estate taxes bring into their treasuries less than the maximum credit for state death taxes allowed by the federal tax law, then the amount payable to the state is automatically increased to absorb the difference. For example, assume that the maximum credit allowed against the federal estate tax for state death taxes amounts to $3,600. Yet the total state death taxes amount to only $3,000. Most states impose an additional estate tax so that they, rather than the federal government, get the extra $600.

4

Joint Ownership of Property

Typically, married couples have the title to their home and other real estate in joint ownership. Frequently there are also joint bank accounts, stocks, bonds, ownership of personal property, and other assets. There are several types of concurrent ownership methods that can be utilized. The most commonly used are:

1. *Tenancies by the Entirety.* A tenancy by the entirety exists only where the coowners are husband and wife. When either spouse dies, the survivor becomes the sole owner by right of survivorship. The right of survivorship cannot be destroyed during the lives of the coowners except with the consent of both. In some states, this form of ownership exists only with respect to real property; in a few states it may exist in the case of personal property.

2. *Joint Tenancies.* Joint tenancies are not limited to husband and wife; however, the two forms of ownership are similar in that the right of survivorship exists in each. Upon the death of one joint owner the property automatically passes to the surviving joint tenant by operation of law. In a joint tenancy one of the coowners may transfer

his or her undivided interest in the property during his or her lifetime.

3. *Tenancies in Common.* In a tenancy in common, which is not limited to husband and wife, there is no right of survivorship. Each owns undivided interests in the property. Either coowner may dispose of his or her undivided interest in the property during his or her life, or by will. When one coowner dies, his or her interest does not go to the surviving coowner, but to the decedent's heirs or according to will.

4. *Community Property.* Community property is created through acquisition during marriage in those states which have a community property system which is derived from the Spanish and French law. Generally, property acquired by the married couple belongs to both no matter who pays the considerations. There are certain exceptions—property acquired by inheritance, gift, etc. Community property laws, where they exist, vary. It is advisable to check your state law. The community property states are Arizona, California, Idaho, Louisiana, Nevada, New Mexico, Texas, and Washington.

Joint ownership of personal property—bank accounts, savings accounts, cars, stocks, bonds, cash, furniture, and other tangible items—has been referred to as a "substitute for a will." Joint ownership should not be thought of as merely a substitute for a will; however, in a nontaxable estate it certainly does eliminate a great deal of troubles with the unnecessary expenses, fees, delays, and frustration of the probate system. In large taxable estates professional advice may be needed to accommodate the effect of the operation of law in the disposition of property.

A married couple with a nontaxable estate—less than $525,625—might well consider structuring ownership of most family assets jointly. In the case of simultaneous death, the wills of both spouses can provide for contingent trusts so that the family assets can be employed for the benefit of the children until they come of age. Life insurance designations can also be structured so that payments are made to designated trusts for the benefit of the children.

Determination of Ownership

The new laws have substantially changed the rule applicable to joint property and has created two rules: one applicable to joint property owned by husbands and wives acquired after 1976; and another rule applicable to all other jointly owned property.

Any property held by a decedent at the time of his or her death as a tenant by the entirety or as a joint tenant with a right of survivorship, other than qualified joint interests with the spouse, will be included in the decedent's gross estate unless it can be proved that the consideration for the joint property was provided by the surviving cotenant or some other party. If part of the consideration was provided by the decedent and part was provided by his surviving cotenant, the percentage of consideration provided by the surviving cotenant will be excluded from the decedent's gross estate. Of course, if all the consideration was provided by the surviving cotenant, the entire property is excluded from the decedent's gross estate.

If the decedent and his cotenant had received their joint interests from a third party as a gift or inheritance, only the decedent's percentage-share interest in the property will be included in his gross estate. The burden of proving that the surviving cotenant or another person contributed to the payment of the consideration for the joint property is on the decedent's estate. The decedent's executor must be able to trace the source of the consideration paid for the property, if any part of the property is to be excluded from the decedent's gross estate. The general result of this rule in many cases is that joint property is included in the gross estate of the first tenant to die simply because of a failure of proof on the part of the executor. This is consistent with what was said earlier about your keeping accurate records of all family transactions.

Husband and Wife, Qualified Joint Interest, and Fractional Share Rule

Only one half of the value of qualified jointly owned

property acquired by husbands and wives after 1976 can be included in the decedent's gross estate, regardless of which spouse furnished the consideration. To qualify, or to change the pre-1977 tenancy to a qualified joint interest with spouse, the following four requirements must be met:

1. The joint interest must be created by one or both spouses after 1976.
2. For personal property, the creation of the joint interest must have been a completed gift and reported for gift tax purposes.
3. For real estate, an election to treat the creation of the joint interest as a taxable gift must have been made and reported for gift tax purposes at the time.
4. Only the husband and wife may be joint owners.

The Tax Reform Act of 1976 provided that the donor spouse of a joint tenancy created before 1977 could elect the 50-50 rule by severing the existing joint tenancy and recreating it in the desired form. This transaction is subject to gift tax. The Revenue Act of 1978 made this easier for a transition period. No severance and re-creation was necessary if the donor spouse reported a gift of the property of a gift tax return filed during any quarter in 1977, 1978, or 1979. The amount of the gift generally is equal to the appreciation attributable to the gift portion of the consideration furnished by the donor spouse at the time of the creation of the joint interest.

5

Major Factors in Your Estate Planning

You must evaluate your family situation to properly formulate your own goals and objectives based upon your current estate and your projected estate. You need to know basic information about the tax laws—income taxes, transfer taxes, sales taxes, estate taxes, inheritance taxes, and others. You should know all the ramifications of joint ownership, ownership through trusts, corporations, partnerships, or other entities; and the effects of community property laws. One of the major considerations in estate planning is a properly prepared and executed will that is kept current by periodic review.

Finally, there are a host of other factors that you must consider which are discussed in this chapter. While it is not necessary to utilize all of these factors, you should know about them in the event any should become important in your estate planning later. For instance, if you are self-employed your interests will be considerably different from those of a person who is employed by a company with a permanent pension and profit sharing plan. What follows can help you take advantage of the best plan which may be available to you.

Life Insurance

The proceeds of life insurance can ordinarily be included in the gross estate of the insured for estate tax purposes when the proceeds are receivable by the estate of the insured or when the insured possessed at his or her death any of the incidents of ownership in the policy. The term "incidents of ownership" has not been clearly defined by the courts; however, the Treasury regulations set out certain examples. These include the right to change the beneficiary, to surrender or cancel the policy, or the right of the insured or his or her estate to receive the economic benefits of the policy.

A reversionary interest in the policy is an incident of ownership where the insured retains a reversionary interest in the policy or its proceeds. This will result irrespective of whether the interest arises from the written terms of the policy or other instrument or by operation of law. The value of the reversionary interest, valued immediately before death, must exceed 5 percent of the value of the policy in order for the rule to apply.

Where the insurance proceeds are large and may have the effect of increasing the estate to a taxable amount, it may be appropriate to consider ways of eliminating the proceeds from the gross estate. The usual methods for accomplishing this are:

1. Assign the policies irrevocably to other persons, such as members of your family;

2. Assign the policies irrevocably to a trust;
3. Arrange for ownership of the policies by your business or employer;
4. Carry the policies as part of a qualified employee benefit plan; or
5. Elect during life to receive the cash value of the policies and use it up or otherwise transfer it from your estate.

One final problem is involved here: a gift of a life insurance policy with a cash value of $3,000 or less, or a term policy with a paid up premium of $3,000 or less made within three years of death can be included in the gross estate. If the incidents of ownership were relinquished more than three years before death, insurance proceeds will not be included in the gross estate. However, premiums paid by the decedent in excess of $3,000 for a donee in a calendar year, after the assignment and within three years of death can be included.

One of the "practical" problems in assigning ownership of insurance policies on your life to your spouse is that when, and if, marital discord causes changes in the marital relationship, problems can surface. On the other hand, insurance policies of all kinds owned by a corporation under your control have much more flexibility.

Group Insurance

A common way for an employee or other person to get the proceeds of his or her group insurance out of his gross estate is to assign all incidents of ownership to the beneficiary. He or she must be careful to also assign the right to convert the insurance to a cash value policy if he or she leaves his job or the group policy is terminated. Such an assignment will be recognized for estate tax purposes provided both the policy and state law specifically permit such an assignment. Practically all states and most group policies specifically permit such assignments. The power of an employee to cancel his or her insurance by quitting the job is not an incident of ownership in the group policy which will cause the proceeds to be included in the estate.

Insurance Owned by a Corporation

Where a corporation owns insurance on the life of its sole or controlling stockholder, the incidents of ownership in the policy will generally be attributed to the stockholder. The proceeds go to his or her estate unless the corporation is beneficiary of the policy or the proceeds are payable to a third party for a valid business purpose. Where the corporation is partial beneficiary and the controlling stockholder's spouse or other named beneficiary gets the rest, the portion not paid to the corporation is part of the controlling stockholder's estate.

In summary, your problem in getting insurance on your life out of your taxable estate is to avoid the gift tax and the transfer within three years of death. Insurance on your life held by a corporation owned or controlled by you may be the best of all worlds—the costs and the proceeds can be handled in a way to avoid income taxes and estate and gift taxes. However, just as in other estate planning matters, you should plan ahead to take advantage of all opportunities for proper estate plan structuring.

Community Property

Community property is that property acquired by either spouse during marriage, other than by gift, devise, or descent. It is based upon the doctrine that property acquired during marriage belongs to the marital community. Generally community property is included in a decedent's gross estate only to the extent of the decedent's interest under the community property state laws.

Community property removed to a common law state retains some or all of its community characteristics under the law prevailing in a common law state. Dower and curtesy interests, or any interest of the surviving spouse created by statute in place of dower and curtesy, are included in the gross estate for allowance of marital deduction for property passing to a surviving spouse. Community income is taxed one half to each spouse regardless of whether they file joint or separate returns. At the death of either spouse, the entire community property may get a stepped up basis, depending on whether at least one half of the property was taxable in the decedent's estate.

There is no gift at the time property which is earned or acquired by one spouse automatically takes on the characteristics of community property. There may be a gift where one spouse's separate property is transformed into community property. Where community property is transformed into separate property, there may be a gift as determined by state law. Where spouses make an inter vivos gift of community property to a third person, both spouses are subject to the gift tax on the value of their respective half interests.

As a general rule, one half of the community property is included in the estate of a deceased spouse. If the wife dies first, in most community property states, one half of the community property would be in her estate even if her husband alone had earned all the community property. The marital deduction normally does not apply to community property because community property already has its own marital deduction built into its structure. However, if one half of the community property is less than $250,000, the excess is eligible for the marital deduction.

If you live in a community property state, have previously lived there, or may live in one, you should review the laws of that state in connection with your estate planning.

Uniform Gifts to Minors Act

The Uniform Gifts to Minors Act has been adopted in all states. It provides that an adult, while living, may make a gift of certain types of property, such as securities, money, or a life insurance contract to a minor by having it registered in the name of, and/or delivering it to, the custodian for a minor. The minor acquires legal title to the property and the donor retains no direct ownership or interest in the gift. Gifts to minors under this act avoid many of the problems and expenses of other methods of transferring property to a minor such as in direct gifts, trust agreements, guardianship arrangements under the supervision of a court.

In order to do this under the statutes it is generally required that you transfer the property to a custodian who holds it for the minor child under your state Gifts to Minors Act. If there are two or more children to whom a parent wishes to make gifts, a custodian must be appointed for each child. Once the gift is made a custodial gift is irrevocable. The property must be distributed to the child when he or she reaches the age of majority, usually 18 or 21, or to the estate of the child in the event of death.

There are several reasons for using this statute as a method for transferring property to a minor. The primary ones are:

1. When a parent wishes to make a gift of money or property for a child's benefit without giving it directly to

the child and without having to set up a trust.

2. When a parent would like to shift some of the income tax burden from his or her high tax bracket to a minor child's lower bracket.

3. When the $3,000 annual gift tax exclusion is desired.

4. When a parent would like to reduce the potential estate tax burden by shifting future appreciation in the value of an asset to a child.

Income from any custodial property will be taxed to the minor whether distributed or not, except when it is used to discharge a legal obligation of some other person, for example, a parent's obligation to support a child. Where income produced by a custodial gift relieves an individual such as a parent of legal obligations, the income is taxed to that person.

The gift is one of a present interest and qualifies for the $3,000 annual exclusion. The exclusion will be allowed even if state law has lowered the age of majority to 18 and custodial property may be distributed to the donee at that age.

The value of property transferred will be included in the estate of a deceased minor-donee. So if the donee dies, assets in the custodial account will be included in his or her estate. However, custodial property will be in the estate of the donor if the donor appoints himself or herself as custodian and dies while serving in that capacity. Likewise, if the donor's spouse dies while serving as custodian and the donor becomes successor and then the donor dies, the value of the property transferred will be part of the donor's estate.

Any gift affected by the $3,000 annual gift tax exclusion, will be automatically excluded from a donor's estate even if the donor dies within three years of making the gift. The gift and income earned by the gift escape income, gift, and estate taxation; that is, the donee, not the donor, is taxed on the income earned by the gift property. The property is not subject to gift taxes, and will not be included in the gross estate of the donor nor will it be considered an adjusted taxable gift.

Section 2503(c) Trusts

Section 2503(c) of the Internal Revenue Code makes provision for gifts to minors in trust. While many direct gifts and gifts under the Uniform Gifts to Minors Act are made there are some objections to these transfers in some situations. Brokers are reluctant to deal in securities owned by minors since they may disaffirm a purchase of stock at any time during their minority. Property titled in a minor's name is to a large extent frozen. A minor's signature on a real estate deed gives the buyer no assurance of permanent title. Moreover, guardianship must be used to avoid many of the objections of an outright transfer to a minor, but a guardian must generally post bond and account periodically to a local court.

Section 2503(c) Trusts can avoid these objections if the requirements of the code are followed. A gift to a minor through a Section 2503(c) Trust will not be considered a gift of a future interest if the income and principal may be expended by or on behalf of the beneficiary at any time prior to the time the beneficiary reaches age 21, and the gift will qualify for the $3,000 annual gift tax exclusion.

Unexpended income and principal must be payable to the beneficiary upon reaching age 21. If the child dies before age 21, the trust corpus must go to the minor's estate or appointee under his or her will. Even if the minor is legally unable to exercise a power or to execute a will because he or she is under age 21 or 18, this fact will not cause the transfer to fail to satisfy the above conditions. In addition, it is permissible to provide that the trust will continue beyond the donee's twenty-first birthday, as long as any time after reaching age 21, the donee can obtain the property in the trust at his or her choice. Thus, the trust property can be distributed to the donee at any time after reaching majority.

A gift through this kind of trust is usually made when the grantor's income tax bracket is high and the donee's income tax bracket is relatively low. Another situation is where the grantor owns an asset which is likely to appreciate substantially over a period of time, but the donor does not want the appreciation in the gross estate. If the income of the trust is distributed each year it is taxable to the donee. Accumulated income is taxed to the trust. The annual $3,000 gift exclusion applies and the appreciation on property placed in trust will be removed from the grantor's gross estate. However, the entire amount will be in the grantor's estate if the grantor is the trustee at the time of his or her death; therefore, you should make sure that another person acts as trustee in situations where you wish to avoid estate taxes.

Keogh Plans For Self-employed Individuals

The Internal Revenue Code provides that a self-employed individual may take a tax deduction for money he or she sets aside for retirement in a Keogh Plan. The term "self-employed" includes a sole proprietor and partners owning 10 percent or more of an interest in a partnership. The Code allows that employees working for self-employed individuals may also participate in the Plan.

A self-employed individual who is an owner-employee with full-time employees must include them in any retirement plan established in which the owner-employee is a participant. Full-time employees with less than three years of service may be excluded, and seasonal or part-time employees may be excluded. A seasonal or part-time employee is one who works less than 1000 hours during a 12 month period. Contributions made for covered employees must be nonforfeitable at the time they are made. Nonforfeitable rights, sometimes called "vested rights," means that whatever is put into the plan for an employee cannot ever be taken away or lost except for death before retirement.

A Keogh Plan must be in writing. The plan can be described in an individually drafted trust instrument, or in a master, or prototype plan. A *master plan* refers to a standardized form of plan, with or without a trust, administered by an insurance company or bank acting as the funding medium for purposes of providing benefits on a standardized basis. In a master plan, the sponsoring organization both funds the benefits and administers the plan. A *prototype plan* refers to a standardized form of plan which is made available by the sponsoring organization for use without change by a self-employed individual who wishes to adopt the plan. A prototype plan will not be administered by the sponsoring organization. The employer administers the plan. Internal Revenue Service approval of the plan is generally sought by the sponsoring organization.

The owner-employee must make a contribution in order to initiate the plan. There are several reasons for using these plans, the most important of which are tax considerations. Contributions made on behalf of an owner-employee to a Keogh Plan are deductible from gross income. The deductible deposits made by an employer are not currently taxable either to the employer himself or to participating employees. No tax will be paid until benefits are actually or constructively received.

Income earned by assets in the plan accumulates tax free. A lump sum distribution receives basically the same tax treatment that a similar distribution would receive from a corporate pension plan. The death benefit payable under a Keogh Plan is estate tax free if receivable by any beneficiary, other than the executor; and if payable as an annuity or other than as a lump sum distribution. A maximum deductible contribution is limited to a lesser of 15 percent of earned income or $7,500. Only the first $100,000 of earned income is considered in applying this limitation. This equals a 7.5 percent contribution rate for an individual deducting the $7,500 maximum. A minimum deductible contribution is permitted to a Keogh Plan of the lesser of 100 percent of earned income or $750 providing the self-employed's adjusted gross income doesn't exceed $15,000 for the year.

An owner-employee may make nondeductible voluntary contributions in addition to his deductile contribution, equal to the lesser of 10 percent of his earned income or $2,500. This assumes his plan also covers a nonowner employee partner or one or more common-law employees who are also permitted to make contributions up to 10 percent of earned income or compensation. A 6 percent nondeductible excise tax is imposed on excess contributions made by self-employed individuals for their own accounts. However where a Keogh Plan is fully insured, the owner-employee may contribute an amount based on average deductible amounts for the three years immediately preceding the year the last contract under the plan was issued without fear of excess contributions tax. The deduction is based on earned income for the tax year.

If an owner-employee receives a distribution from his plan before reaching the age of 59½, a tax of 10 percent of the amount of the taxable distribution is imposed in addition to the normal tax on any gain. Exemptions apply for distributions due to the employee's death or disability. Employees can withdraw voluntary contributions, but not the income earned by those contributions, at any time prior to retirement without penalty.

Individual Retirement Savings Plan—IRA

Recent changes in the Internal Revenue Code permit individuals who are not actively participating in a qualified or governmental pension plan, profit sharing plan, Keogh plan, or tax deferred annuity to establish their own savings plan. Under this provision of the code, a person can set up an individual retirement account (IRA) and take a deduction from gross annual income equal to the lesser of $1,500 or 15 percent of compensation or earned income.

An individual who has a nonworking spouse may

contribute up to $1,750—that is, $875 for each or 15 percent of compensation if lower. This can be done by establishing separate accounts, or subaccounts, for the self-employed individual and spouse.

The requirements for setting up an IRA are relatively simple. You have the option to set aside retirement savings in an annuity contract, certain life insurance endowment contracts, a trusteed or custodial account with a bank, savings and loan association, credit union, or a special U.S. Government bond. In some circumstances you can split the total contributions into two separate accounts. Contributions can be made by the individual, the employer and his or her union. They must be in cash and may be as late as 45 days after the close of the taxable year. This gives most taxpayers until February 14 in which to make contributions.

If you and your spouse are both working and not covered under a qualified plan this is even better in terms of the amount that can be contributed. All contributions made to your IRA account, within the limits set by the code, are deductible from gross income, and the earnings of the account accumulate tax free. In order to receive IRA payments without tax penalty the individual must be at least 59½ years of age. A penalty of 10 percent of the amount of the distribution is levied on premature distributions. When distributions are made they are taxed at ordinary income tax rates—usually in a lower tax bracket.

The federal estate and gift tax exclusions applicable to qualified corporate retirement plans are now available to the individual retirement accounts. Payments are excluded from estate taxes if the payments are made to beneficiaries other than the estate, and the survivor's interest is paid in the form of an annuity. An annuity can be of the commercial type or any other arrangement which provides for a series of substantially equal periodic payments. Substantially equal means that payments must be spread out over the survivor's lifetime or over a period of at least 36 months after the decedent's death. The three year payment provision must be elected by the date the federal estate tax return is filed or, if earlier, the date the return is required to be filed after taking the allowed extensions into account. This estate tax exclusion applies only to the extent the death benefit is attributable to deductible or rollover contributions. No exclusion is allowed for the portion of a death benefit attributable to contributions which were nondeductible.

Redemption of Corporation Stock under Section 303 of the Internal Revenue Code

Section 303 of the Internal Revenue Code provides that a redemption of the stock included in a decedent's estate for federal tax purposes is to be considered a distribution in exchange for the stock, not a taxable dividend. This is to the extent that the distribution does not exceed the amount of federal and state death taxes, interest on those taxes, and the deductible funeral and administration expenses of the estate. At the time of the redemption, if the value of the stock redeemed is greater than the carry over basis, there will be a capital gain tax on the appreciation. To avoid the dividend treatment, it is necessary to meet specifications which are laid down by law as follows:

1. The stock redeemed must be included in the decedent's gross estate.

2. The redemption must be made from any shareholder who has the burden of paying the death taxes and funeral and administration expenses. Wills should be prepared so the stock to be redeemed is not part of the marital deduction share.

3. The federal estate tax value of all the stock of the corporation whose stock is redeemed, which is included in determining the value of the decedent's gross estate, must be more than 50 percent of the adjusted gross estate (gross estate less deductions for administration expenses, debts, taxes and losses and before the marital deduction).

4. The stock of two or more corporations is treated as the stock of a single corporation for the purpose of computing whether the stock makes up the required percentage of the gross or taxable estate provided more than 75 percent in value of the outstanding stock of

49

each corporation is included in the gross estate. In meeting this 75 percent requirement, you can include the surviving spouse's interest in stock held by the spouse and the decedent together as community property.

5. Redemptions qualify only in the combined amount of the following:

   a. Death taxes imposed because of the decedent's death, plus interest thereon. This includes federal and state estate, inheritance, legacy and succession taxes, and similar foreign taxes.

   b. The amount of the funeral and administration expenses allowable as deductions for federal estate tax purposes.

Normally the redemption must take place within the period of limitations provided in the code for the assessment of the federal estate tax or within 90 days after the expiration of this period. This gives three years and ninety days after filing the estate tax return, irrespective of any extension of the period for assessment. The redemption may be extended as long as 15 years after death if the estate qualifies under the code for extension of time payment of estate tax. The value of the closely held business must exceed 65 percent of the adjusted gross estate. If the decedent has more than one business, the estate can meet the 65 percent test if he had more than 20 percent interest in each business. There are special rules which limit the amount of qualifying redemption distributions that are made more than four years after the decedent's death.

Sub Chapter S Corporation

If you are a small business owner or wish to form your own corporation for any purpose you should consider electing the use of the Sub Chapter S taxation available under the code. The code permits shareholders in certain qualified corporations to elect to pass the taxation through to the shareholders. Income is taxed directly to the shareholders whether distributed or not. They report the income but benefit by the corporation's long term capital gain and net operating loss, which are passed through to them. Shareholders are able to take investment tax credits. If you form your own corporation you should also take advantage of Section 1244 stock issue. (See *Form Your Own Corporation*, another publication in this series.)

Only a "small business corporation" may elect the special tax treatment. As a general rule, a small business corporation is one that meets the following requirements:

1. It must be a domestic corporation.
2. It does not have more than 15 shareholders.
3. All shareholders must be individuals, estates, or certain types of trusts.
4. No nonresident alien may be a shareholder.

5. The corporation may issue only one class of stock—voting common stock.

6. The corporation may not earn in excess of 80 percent of its gross receipts from sources outside the United States.

7. The corporation may not earn in excess of 20 percent of its gross receipts from interest, dividends, rents, royalties, annuities, and gains from sales or exchanges of securities.

How To Elect Sub Chapter S Tax Status

It is quite simple to make the election. You merely complete Form 2553 and file it with the IRS. A valid election can be made only if all shareholders consent. This can be done at any time during the entire preceding year and the first 75 days of the election year. Once election is made, it is effective for all later years, unless it is terminated.

The election will be terminated in any one of the following circumstances:

1. A new shareholder affirmatively refuses to consent to the election within 60 days after becoming a shareholder.

2. All the shareholders consent to its revocation.

3. The corporation fails to meet any of the qualifications listed above.

When an election has been terminated or revoked, a

new election cannot be made for five years, unless the IRS consents to an earlier election.

The corporation has no income tax; however, it is required to file a return on Form 1120S each tax year. Each shareholder is required to show his or her share of earnings in individual tax returns.

$5,000 Employees Death Benefit Exclusion

The estate or other beneficiary of an employee can receive, tax free, up to $5,000 from the decedent's employer. This exclusion applies to the beneficiary of any employee of a corporation, a sole proprietorship, or a partnership (but is not available to beneficiaries of partners or sole proprietors). The income tax exclusion is available regardless of whether the benefit is paid voluntarily or under contract, whether paid directly or to a trust, and whether paid on a lump sum or in installments. The exclusion will be allowed regardless of whether the benefit is paid to a former or to an active employee.

Orphan's Exclusion

The orphan's exclusion is similar to the marital deduction. A deduction is allowed for the value of property that passes, at death, to a decedent's child under the age of 21 when there is no surviving spouse of decedent or other known parent. The deduction is allowed to an estate of an adoptive parent even though one or both of the natural parents are known and surviving.

To qualify, the property must be included in the decedent's gross estate and the child must receive the property or interest. The maximum deduction allowable is $5,000 multiplied by the excess of 21 over the child's age on the date of the decedent's death. For example, if the child is eight years of age at the decedent's death, the deduction would be 13 x $5,000 = $65,000. The amount of deduction is limited to the amount actually passing from the decedent to the child. If it is not left outright to the child, it can be left in trust for him or her, as long as the terms qualify under the rules for the marital deduction under the code (relating to life estates or other terminable interests left to a surviving spouse). Therefore, the child must eventually receive the property or have a power of appointment over it. The interest will not be treated as a terminable interest if the property passes to another person due to the child's death before the youngest child of the decedent reaches the age of 21.

The Private Annuity

A private annuity is an arrangement between two parties in which the transferor conveys complete ownership of property to the transferee in exchange for the promise to make periodic payments to the transferor for a period of time. Typically, the period is the transferor's life or the life of the survivor of the transferor and the spouse.

There are two types of private annuities: the single life annuity under which payments cease at the death of the annuitant; and the joint and last survivor annuity, in which payments continue until the death of the last survivor, (for example, payments continue as long as either the husband or wife is alive). Since payments under this type of arrangement will continue for longer than payments under a single life annuity, the amounts paid each year will be less than that payable under a single life annuity.

A private annuity should be considered for use when you have one or more of these situations:

1. When you have a need to spread capital gains.
2. When you wish to retire and shift control of a business to a family member or to a key employee.
3. When you desire to remove a sizable asset, such as a business, from your estate for estate tax purposes.
4. When you wish to obtain a fixed retirement income.
5. When you won a large parcel of nonincome producing property but want to make it income producing.
6. Any other situation where you wish to convey property to others with long term payments. The private annuity has many advantages over the installment sale.

There are certain requirements under the Internal Revenue Code for setting up a private annuity. Although any type of property can be used, income producing property is the most appropriate. For the plan to be successful it is necessary for the transferee to be in a financial condition to make payments during the period of the annuity. If the transferee has substantial independent income, then almost any asset can serve as the property to be transferred. However, if the transferee does not have sufficient income or resources to make the payments then the property sold should be either income producing or at least should be of a type that the transferee can use it to generate income.

This is important because the transferee's promise to make the payments must be unsecured. If the promise of the transferee is secured a taxable event will occur immediately upon the transfer, and the transferor would be required to pay tax on the full amount of the gain. The gain would be the difference between the amount realized and the transferor's adjusted basis in the property.

The transferee should be a person not regularly engaged in issuing private annuities. The transferee is usually a family member, key employee, or other persons who are the natural object of the transferor's bounty. For example, most private annuities are made between parents and children. The annuity amount must be determined by measuring the value and cost basis of the property. This may require an appraisal by independent experts. The transferor is usually in a high estate tax bracket and wishes to reduce his or her estate and provide himself or herself with a lifetime income.

The procedure for arranging a private annuity is quite simple. You should draw up a written agreement for the sale of property in return for the payment by the transferee. The payments must be based upon actuarial tables and relate to the age of the transferor or other recipient of the payments.

There are many tax advantages to this arrangement. For federal estate tax purposes, where the annuity ceases at the death of the transferor, the value of the property sold to the transferee in return for his promise to pay the annuity is excludible from the transferor's estate. This is because property sold by a decedent for full and adequate consideration before death is not taxable in his or her estate. The value of the promised payment will be excludible. This is because the selling price in a private annuity arrangement is an income which will expire upon the annuitant's death. However, this is not the case with a joint and survivor annuity.

In a joint and last survivor annuity, payments will continue until the death of the last survivor. Therefore, if the transferor's spouse survives, the present value of future payments to him or her will be includible in the transferor's estate (assuming he or she was sole owner of the property that was transferred in return for the joint and survivor annuity payments).

Each annuity payment made by the transferee to the transferor is treated partially as a tax free return of capital, partially as a capital gain, and the balance as ordinary income. The transferee is not allowed a deduction for any payments made to the transferor.

There will be no gift if the annual payments made by the transferee to the transferor are actuarially determined to be equal to the amount of the property sold. However, if the value of the promise made by the transferee is less than the value of the property transferred, the difference will constitute a gift by the transferor.

The following form is an example of a private annuity agreement.

FORM 1: Private Annuity Agreement

This Annuity Agreement is made this, the ____ day of _____ , 19__ , by and between _____ , of _____ , hereinafter called Transferor, and her son, _____ , also of _____ _____ , hereinafter called the Transferee.

Whereas, Transferor is the owner of that certain real estate situate, lying and being in _____ County, State of _____ , and in the City of _____ , thereof numbered on the official plats of said City as all of _____ . There is situate on said real property an apartment house.

Whereas, Transferor is 60 years of age and wishes to be free of the liabilities of the management of real property and wishes to be assured of a fixed annual income for the remainder of her life, regardless of whether such property is rented.

Whereas, the market value of said property is $ _____ according to an appraisal made by the _____ Real Estate Board and Transferor's basis in said property is $ _____ ; and

Whereas, Transferee wishes to acquire said property as an investment and is willing to make fixed annual payments of $ _____ for the remainder of Transferor's life in exchange for said property.

COVENANTS AND AGREEMENTS

Now Therefore, for and in consideration of the mutual promises made by each party to the other and of the mutual agreements contained herein, the parties hereto agree with each other as follows:

1. The Transferor shall this day execute and deliver to the Transferee a good and sufficient Warranty Deed conveying all of her right, title, and interest in and to the above described real property in _____ . Transferor shall pay all costs in connection with the preparation of the Deed and the transfer tax due the State of _____ .

2. Transferee, for himself, his heirs, and legal representatives does hereby agree to pay to the Transferor the sum of $ _____ for her lifetime, payable the ____ day of _____ ; the first payments to be made on _____ .

3. The parties agree that taxes, insurance, and rentals shall be prorated as of the ____ day of _____ , 19__ . Transferee shall pay all expenses in connection with the title examination and survey he has caused to be made in connection with his acquisition of said property. He shall also pay all recording fees.

4. The aforesaid payments to the Transferor are to be made without reference to the transferred property and irrespective of any income earned by the property. These payments are obligations of the Transferee and are not limited in any way to the value of the property.

5. The Transferee is given the right to sell, transfer, assign, or pledge the property free and clear of any claims whatsoever by the Transferor and it is understood that the payments to be made to the Transferor are not secured by the property.

This agreement shall inure to the benefit of and shall be binding upon the Transferee's heirs and legal representatives.

In Witness Whereof this Annuity Agreement is signed, sealed, and delivered in duplicate on the day and year first herein written, it being agreed that each copy of this Agreement shall constitute an original.

Signed, sealed and
delivered in the
presence of: (as to
Transferor)

_____
Transferor

Signed, sealed and
delivered in the
presence of: (as to
Transferee)

_____
Transferee

Rights of the Spouse and Children

One of the overriding matters that you must keep in mind in your estate planning is the effect of your state statutes on the statutory rights of your spouse and children. Each state has a provision that protects spouses and children in certain circumstances. While the statutes have a formula for the distribution of all property in the absence of a will or other disposition by the testator, there are certain rights that cannot be defeated by a testator. In order to give you a better understanding of this subject it is helpful to give a very brief summary of the history and background to the structure of the current statutes which include such items as dower, curtesy, homestead, community property, family allowances, and exempt property. By whatever name the particular statute may employ, there has developed a thread in all the statutes which places certain limitations on the rights or power of a married person to deny property rights to a surviving spouse.

Dower and Curtesy

In most states, the spouse is entitled to a specified minimum percentage or a certain part of the estate. If a married person attempts to leave his or her spouse less than the statutory share, the surviving spouse has a right to elect to take against the will. Other states have retained the common law rights of dower and curtesy or an equivalent statutory right. An elective share may or may not be equivalent to an intestate share. An elective share is usually, but not always, in addition to family allowances and homestead rights.

The Uniform Probate Code suggests a provision that if the married person dies, the surviving spouse has a right of election to take an elective share of one-third (1/3) of the augmented estate. The *augmented estate* is the estate reduced by funeral and administrative expenses, homestead allowance, family allowances, and exemptions, and enforceable claims, but with the addition of the value of property transferred by the decedent to third parties, during the marriage, in specified ways, and certain other adjustments.

Strictly speaking *dower* means the legal right or interest the wife acquires by marriage in the estate of her husband. At common law it consists in the use, during her natural life after the death of her husband, of one-third of all the real estate which her husband acquired during the marriage.

Dower has been called the rights of widows in husband's real estate created by statutory enactments. Dower sometimes includes personal property as well as real property. It is the provision which the law makes for the sustenance of the widow for the nurture and education of her young children after the death of her husband. *Curtesy*, historically, was a life estate of the husband in the real property his wife owned during marriage.

Common law dower has been abolished in England and in most of the states in America. In those states where it has been retained, it is seldom exactly the same in any two states. Each state statute is different as to what lands are dowable and in almost all aspects of the definitions of the rights. The statutory rights of surviving spouses, based, as it is on the old common law rights of dower and curtesy, are also different from state to state. In all events it is essential for you to know about these statutes because they can make a significant difference in the ultimate disposition of your estate.

Each state has such a statutory provision, and whether it is called dower, curtesy, statutory share, homestead, or some other name, it is a fixed share (usually from 1/3 to 1/2) of the estate which cannot be defeated by will or otherwise (with some exceptions). The eight states which have community property laws are most favorable to surviving spouses.

6

Writing Your Own Will as a Part of Your Estate Planning

A properly prepared will, reviewed periodically to accommodate changes, is a vital part of any family, financial, or estate plan. In preparing a will there are several major objectives to accomplish. Protection and planning for each member of your family is the most important. This may include extensive discussions with the adult members of your family and a consideration of the needs of each family member. Full attention should be given to the temperament and values of each family member, the ability of each to contribute to his own support, the skill of each in handling money, and the education, social, and vocational objectives of each. These discussions should be preliminary to the preparation and execution of any will whether it is for you, your spouse, or any other member of your family.

Minimizing taxes is another important objective that should be included in the overall estate plans. The estate taxes, as well as income and gift taxes, should be carefully evaluated and understood so that your family receives all the tax benefits to which they are entitled.

A will must be carefully written to avoid lawsuits, probate contests, or other legal proceedings which may be necessary to clarify any uncertain or ambiguous language in the will. Careful reflection should be given to the selection of the person who will act as executor or executrix. It is advisable to select someone who is willing to undertake the job, who is qualified to handle it; and a person in whom you and other family members repose confidence.

A Checklist is given later to help you organize the information and facts needed to make appropriate decisions about a will. After an analysis of your estate plans and a consideration of the essential factors regarding wills, you can turn to the sample forms, select the one that most nearly meets your needs, and adapt or change the paragraphs (by substitution of alternative paragraphs) to specifically satisfy your personal needs. You will find almost every combination you will need, but feel free to draft a new one in your own language that expresses your true intentions and desires. Be careful not to use words or phrases that are inconsistent, uncertain, or ambiguous. Say it plain and simple.

What Is a Will?

A will is an instrument by which you, the testator, can provide for the disposition of property after death.

After writing and signing a will, you can change it at any time subject to the laws that are in effect at the time as reflected in your state statutes. The object of the statutes governing wills is to enable you to designate how your property is to be disposed of and to insure that your desires and wishes are carried out. This is subject, of course, to the paramount power of the state to regulate the extent and nature of your right to transfer property.

In order to determine whether or not an instrument is a will, the courts will generally look to your intentions at the time the will was written. If you intended to dispose of your estate, the instrument is generally considered testamentary in character. The testamentary character of an instrument is determined by the interpretation of, and from the construction of, the language you use in writing it. If it is clear that your intention is to dispose of your property after your death, the document contains sufficient testamentary character to constitute a will. The courts, in the interpretation of a will, generally consider the instrument as a whole. What property you have and how you intend to dispose of it must be clearly stated in the will. This cannot be done for you after your demise.

Unless there is an intention to dispose of property, there is no will. Unfortunately many people state in wills that they "wish" or "hope" or "desire" that the beneficiaries do certain things with the property in their estate. These words, when used in a will to merely suggest that the property be disposed of in a certain way, are not legally binding. You should not use these words or similar words that do not clearly indicate an intent to dispose of your property. You should avoid such terminology altogether or at least state what you want clearly in writing. Use of this kind of uncertain language is an open invitation to litigation. You must know the contents of your will. It is usually presumed that a person who signs a written instrument knows what is in it, but this is not always the case. Questions regarding these possible issues can be avoided by following the checklist, instructions, and step-by-step procedures that follow. A will written in a language that you do not understand may still be effective if you know and understand the contents. A blind person may validly sign a will if he or she knows and understands the contents of the will and has an intent to dispose of property.

What are the items to be covered in a will? Well, there is no magic formula but the usual terms in a basic will include:

1. A statement identifying the testator;
2. Special instructions on payment of debts, or other such items;
3. Burial instructions and other general matters;
4. Appointment of an executor or executrix;
5. General and special disposition of property;
6. Residuary clause; and

7. Attestation clause with signatures and witnesses. Scandalous or derogatory matters should never be placed in a will as this is an open invitation to unnecessary lawsuits against the estate. If scandalous matter does appear in a will, the courts simply disregard it; it has no effect, function, or purpose.

Do You Need a Will?

It may not be accurate to say that everybody needs a will, but every adult who has any assets or property should seriously consider having one. If a full and complete understanding of the need for a will is known, a will should naturally follow. One purpose of a will is to designate who *shall* receive your assets. Another equally important function of a will is to designate who *shall not* receive your property. You should carefully study the reasons for having or not having a will and make a decision based on an evaluation of the facts and circumstances surrounding your own personal needs.

The reasons for having a will relate to the convenience of handling the administration of the estate; the prompt handling of the immediate needs of a surviving family; the saving of administrative costs and expenses; and assurance that your assets will belong to those whom you have designated. Also, there is the very important matter of transferring an estate to the beneficiaries without having most of it (or a large share of it) paid in taxes.

If you do not have a will that designates an executor or executrix to administer the estate, the probate court will be required to appoint one. This can result in unnecessary delays. An appointed administrator is usually required to post a bond; this is both expensive and time consuming. In addition to the expenditure of unnecessary bond premiums, the estate is charged with legal fees for the attorney who handles the procedural activities. A properly prepared will that designates an executor and waives bond (where appropriate) would eliminate these delays and expenses.

Where there is no will and the court appoints an administrator, the mere sale of assets of the estate usually required court authorization. Moreover, an appointed administrator would probably be required to obtain an appraisal of property before making a sale. If there are minor children involved, it may be necessary to have the court appoint a legal guardian to protect the children's interests. A properly prepared will can avoid most of these expenses and delays.

Finally, depending upon the size of your estate, there may be an assessment of estate taxes which might have been reduced or avoided by a will and a good estate plan. Those who complain about the high cost of probate, should realize that poor estate planning and the failure to have a will, or having a poorly drafted will, can contribute as much to the unnecessary costs of probate as the inefficient, ineffective, and slow "probate system."

Almost everyone should have a will. Here are some cases that dramatically illustrate the importance and necessity for having wills.

Case 1

John, a 34 year old widower, had two daughters, Ann, 6, and Linda, age 4. John married Betty, 30, and revised his will leaving his entire estate to his new wife, assuming that in case of his death Betty would take care of her stepdaughters.

Shortly thereafter, John and Betty were fatally injured in an automobile crash. John died instantly and Betty died two days later. All of John's property went to Betty in accordance with the directions of his will; Betty had no will. Under the state statutes all of John's property and all of Betty's property went to Betty's relatives. Ann and Linda were not related to Betty by blood and they got nothing.

Case 2

Jim, 35, is married to Martha, age 34, and they have two children ages 5 and 8. Jim's father and mother are both living and he has four brothers and two sisters all of whom he loves. His estate is in excess of $300,000; he has given Martha jewelry, furs, and other gifts from time to time; his will leaves everything to Martha. Martha has no will.

Jim's mother-in-law, age 67, is a battle-ax and he

71

does not like her—and she does not like him. On a vacation trip an accident resulted in the instant death of Jim and his two children; Martha died two weeks later. The mother-in-law probably gets everything, and Jim's family gets nothing.

Case 3

Mona, age 34, married Jake, 36. Neither had a will. They had no children, and are separated after a series of bitter fights. Mona dislikes Jake and hates his mother, Angela. Mona's mother, 74, inherited $300,000 from Mona's father who died one year ago. Mona's mother dies and leaves the entire estate to Mona; five days later Mona dies in an accident and Jake was killed in a barroom brawl just a few days later. In this situation a major part of the estate of Mona's father will be consumed in administration expenses, estate taxes, and litigation expenses. If anything is left after the "probate" proceedings, it will probably go to Angela.

When you have a properly prepared and executed will, you will have a sense of pride, satisfaction, and well being in knowing you have done the right thing. Do not, however, become complacent or forget the will entirely once you have written it. You should review your will and estate plans at regular intervals. When there is a significant change in your estate, family, or personal situation, the appropriate changes should be made in your will to accommodate these changes.

What May Happen if You Do Not Have a Will?

If you die without a will, your property and assets will be distributed to those persons designated in the statutes of your state regardless of your wishes or desires and wholly aside from the needs of your family members. If you do not have a will, you automatically add to the costs of the probate proceedings.

During my career as a practicing attorney, I have seen millions of dollars diverted from estates to legal fees, court costs, appraisal fees, executors' fees, guardian ad litem fees, expert witness fees, brokers' fees, taxes, tax penalties, interest payments, and other unnecessary expenditures rather than going to the family members as the decedent had wanted. The absence of a will can cause delays, inconvenience, personal sadness, and it frequently results in a miscarriage of justice. All the hidden and repressed bitterness and hostility of every family member seems to surface at these times. A properly prepared will can prevent most of the sadness and unpleasantness indicated by these examples.

If you die without a will, which is legally called intestate or intestacy, your property will probably be distributed in accordance with your state's laws of descent and distribution or intestate succession. These laws are enacted by the legislature based upon the assumption that most people want their estate to go to certain relatives. These assumptions may or may not comply with your personal desires or wishes. Most statutes give first priority to the decedent's spouse, if any, and to natural children, if any. Parents, descendants, brothers, and sisters are usually designated in the absence of a spouse or natural children; other relatives, if any, follow in order. It is beyond the scope of this book to elaborate on the many variations in the statutes, and the complications which can develop in applying them, or the many legal issues generated by litigation in attempts to apply the statutes to particular situations.

Execution and Witnessing of Wills

The proper signing and witnessing of your will is extremely important. Your intentions and wishes are immaterial. If you do not follow the applicable statute your will may not be valid no matter what your wishes may be. Make sure that you understand all of the rules for execution and witnessing of wills.

It is recommended that you make a "ceremony" out of the signing and witnessing of your will so that the witnesses will remember the occasion; that family members or persons who take under the will not act as witnesses; that you have younger persons who are likely to be available when needed; and that you have an extra witness if convenient. Most statutes require at least two witnesses; some require at least three; Louisiana requires more in some circumstances. Most statutes require competent or credible witnesses; some statutes specify certain age requirements for witnesses; most do not. Some states make a devise or bequest to a witness void, with certain exceptions; some do not. A few statutes prohibit persons who have been convicted of perjury or other crimes from being competent witnesses to wills. It can be important for you to have this information available as it applies to your state.

As an extra precaution, it is suggested that you follow all of the following step-by-step procedures, whether or not they are required by your state statutes. These steps are included in the ceremony that many law offices routinely follow in the signing of wills.

Procedures for Signing and Witnessing Wills
Step 1

Prepare the final draft of the will, preferably on a typewriter, with an original and one or more copies. Type the attestation clause in the proper place. Allow ample space for your signature and the signatures and addresses of the witnesses. Number the pages and bind them together firmly. Make sure you thoroughly understand the meaning of every part of your will.

Step 2

Bring the witnesses together. Three witnesses will satisfy the requirements in all states except Louisiana.

None of these witnesses should be related to you or your wife or husband, nor should they be anyone named in any way in your will. You and the witnesses should be in a separate room with no one else in the room.

Step 3

Inform the witnesses that the document before them is your last will. It is not necessary or even desirable that they be allowed to read it. Then you should state that you are about to sign your will and request the witnesses to witness your signature. With the witnesses watching, you should then date the will and sign your name on the line below the date.

After you have completely signed and dated the will, say to the witnesses, "This is my signature and this is my will." Then request that the witnesses sign it. You should sign only the original; the carbon copies, as a matter of good practice, remained unsigned, but conformed.

Step 4

Have the witnesses read the attestation clause. Then have each witness sign immediately below the attestation clause and write his or her address. The witnesses should see you sign the will and you should see them sign it. Neither you nor any of the witnesses should leave the room until all have signed the document. Each signature should be observed by you and all the witnesses.

Step 5

Now the document is a will. The signed original

should be placed in a safe place where it is available to you and the executor. Do not place it in your safety deposit vault because a court order may be required to get it out. The unsigned copies should be placed in a different safe place for information purposes.

The Holographic Wills, the Nuncupative Wills, and the Louisiana Code Wills

When we talk about wills we generally refer to a typewritten, signed, witnessed will with all the information provided by the applicable state statute. However, there are other kinds of special wills that are valid in some circumstances and places.

The Holographic Will

The holographic will is very popular and although it is valid in only 25 state it is anticipated that more states will enact statutes based upon the Uniform Probate Code, which authorizes holographic wills. The nuncupative will is of little or no real value and the Louisiana Code Will is the only you can have in Louisiana which includes a holographic will, called "olographic" in the Lousiana Code.

A holographic will—unwitnessed, unattested, entirely in the testator's handwriting—originated in the French law. Some of the statutes require that the entire will be written, dated, and signed in the testator's own handwriting. Other statutes, based on the Uniform Probate Code, require only that the signature and the material provisions of the will be in the testator's handwriting. By requiring only the "material provisions" to be in the testator's handwriting, such holographic wills may be valid even though immaterial parts such as the date or introductory wording be printed or stamped. Under these statutes a valid holographic will might even be executed on some printed will forms if the printed portion could be eliminated and the handwritten portion could evidence the testator's will. For some persons unable to obtain legal assistance, the holographic will may be adequate. Moreover, many people who can afford legal assistance prefer to do it themselves. If your statute permits holographic wills you may wish to use this easy method. (See Chapter 7.)

The Nuncupative Will

A nuncupative will is one that is not in writing, and exists only when the testator declares his will orally before witnesses. At early common law, it was not essential to the validity of a nuncupative will that the testator be ill, and there were no restrictions on the time of making it. To guard against the frauds for which oral wills seemed to offer so many facilities, provision was made in the original statute of frauds in England that a nuncupative will to be valid must be "made in the time of the last sickness." The privilege of leaving a nuncupative will, it was generally held at that time, was to be exercised as a matter of

78

necessity, not of choice. Although the nuncupative will is still valid in a few states under very limited circumstances, it is not recommended that you rely on it. Some of the restrictions and limitations on these wills are that

1. they are applicable only to a person in imminent peril or death, whether from illness or otherwise, and shall be valid only if the testator died as a result of the impending peril;

2. they occur at the immediate apprehension of death and with no ability to reduce the will to writing;

3. they require two or more witnesses;

4. they are valid as to personal property only;

5. they limit the amount of personal property (usually a few hundred dollars); and

6. they require that the terms of the will must be reduced to writing by a witness within a short period of time (usually a few days or weeks).

The Louisiana Code

The Louisiana Code is based on the French law and has several kinds of wills somewhat different from the other states. There are four classes of wills in Louisiana:

1. Nuncupative or open testaments;

2. mystic or sealed testaments;

3. olographic testaments; and

4. statutory testaments. (C.C. 1574)

Nuncupative Testament

The nuncupative testament by public act must be received by a notary public in the presence of three witnesses residing in the place where the will is executed, or five witnesses not residing in the place. The testament must be written by the notary as it is dictated. It must then be read to the testator in the presence of the witnesses. Express mention must be made of the whole, observing that all the formalities must be fulfilled at one time, without interruption and without turning aside to other acts. The testament must be signed by the testator, or if he does not know how or is not able to sign, express mention of his declaration and of the cause which hinders him to sign must be made in the act. The testament must also be signed by the witnesses or by one for all, if others cannot write.

The nuncupative testament under private signature must be written by the testator himself, or by any other person from his dictation, or even by one of the witnesses, in the presence of five witnesses residing in the place where the will is received or in the presence of seven witnesses residing out of that place. It will suffice if in the presence of the same number of witnesses the testator presents the paper on which he has written his testament or caused it to be written out of their presence, and declare to them that that paper contains his last will and testament. In either case the testament must be read by the testator to the witnesses, or by one of the witnesses to the rest in the presence of the testator. It must be signed by the testator, if he knows how or is able to sign, and by the witnesses, or at least by two of them in case the others know how to sign, and those of the witnesses who do not know how to sign must affix their mark. In the country it suffices for the validity of the nuncupative testament under private signature that the testament be passed in the presence of three witnesses residing in the place where the testament is received, or of five witnesses residing out of the place, provided that in this case a great number of witnesses cannot be had.

Sealed or Mystic Testament

This will may be made by the testator signing his dispositions, whether he has written them himself or has caused them to be written by another person. The paper containing those dispositions, or the paper serving as their envelope must be closed and sealed. The testator must present it, thus closed and sealed, to the notary and to three witnesses or he must cause it to be closed and sealed in their presence. Then he must declare to the notary in the presence of the witnesses, that the paper contains his testament, written by himself, or by another at his direction, and signed by him, the testator. The notary must then draw up the act of superscription which must be written on that paper or the sheet which serves as its envelope, and that act must be signed by the testator, and by the notary and the witnesses. All must be done without interruption or turning aside to other acts. In case the testator, by reason of any hindrance which has happened since the signing of the testament, cannot sign the act of superscription, mention of the declaration made by him must be made, but it is not necessary to increase the number of witnesses. Those who are not able to write or sign their names cannot make dispositions in the form of a mystic testament.

Olographic Testament

A will which is written by the testator himself. In order to be valid it must be entirely written, dated, and signed by the testator without its being subject to any other formality.

Statutory Testament

A statutory testament may be typewritten, printed, or written in any other manner. The testator must signify to notary public and two competent witnesses that the instrument is his will. He must sign his name at the end of the will and on each separate sheet of the instrument. If the testator declares that he is not able to sign because of physical infirmity, express mention and cause thereof must be made in the paper and testator must affix his mark on each sheet of the paper. This will must include just above the signatures of the testator, notary, and the witnesses the following: "Signed (on each page or if not signed by testator, statement of his signification or declaration that he is unable to sign and of the physical cause) and declared (or signified) by the testator above named, in our presence to be his last will and testament, and in the presence of the testator and each other we have hereunto subscribed our names on this ___ day of _____ , 19__ ." Except where due to physical infirmity, persons who do not know or are unable to sign name, or who do not know or are unable to read, cannot make this type of testament. (C.C. 1578, 1579, 1580, 1581, 1582, 1583, 1584, 1585, 1586, 1588)

Witnesses

The following persons are incapable of being witnesses to wills:

1. Persons under the age of sixteen;
2. insane, deaf, dumb, or blind persons;
3. persons whom the criminal laws declare incapable of exercising civil functions;
4. married women to the wills of their husbands. (There are also limitations on heirs or named legatees.)

Revocation of Wills

Almost without exception the average person would have occasion to revoke a will only by writing another will with the typical phrase, "I hereby revoke all wills and codicils heretofore made by me." Few people revoke wills or codicils without immediately making another will or codicil. However, there are those rare occasions when this may be appropriate and the statutes have procedures and rules for the manner in which it may be done.

The statutes set out specific provisions for revoking wills, and these are listed later. Be alert to updating or changing your will in the event of marriage, divorce, annulment, or birth or adoption of children after signing of your will.

Practices and Procedures for Writing Wills

One of the most embarrassing and well founded complaints against attorneys is that the turgid language they use in legal documents leads to perplexity, obscurity, and confusion. This is especially true in the case of wills because attorneys seem obsessed with using the language they learned in law school as though there were some magic to the high-sounding phrases. I must confess that I did this for many years.

For example, I remember the clause, "I give, devise and bequeath all the rest, residue, and remainder of my estate, real, personal, or mixed, whatsoever and wheresoever located, to my beloved wife, Emily Jane Howell, formerly Emily Jane Gifford." Most form books use it, most attorneys I have known use it, but I think it is better to say: "I give the residue of my estate to my wife Jane."

In most of the forms, clauses, and phrases used in this book, I will try to speak in plain English instead of the "lawyer language," and you should feel free to improve upon the simplicity of the language used if you deem it proper. The ultimate objective is for you to write a will which accurately expresses your desires and intentions in the disposition of your property.

How to Write Your Own Will

There is a great myth in our society that one must have a lawyer to prepare a will. You do not always need a lawyer; you can prepare your own will as you can plan your own estate. That is, unless you have (1) some unusual or extraordinary problem, or (2) some tax problem. The basis for the myth is that you don't always know how to determine whether you have one of these "problems." So first, you need to know whether you have one of these problems and if you don't, you can do it yourself; and, second, you need to know how to do it yourself. This part of the book tells you how to answer both of these questions, (1) whether you have problems that require a lawyer or specialist, and (2) how to write your own will.

Almost every lawyer, early in his or her career engages in an in depth research, study, and analysis program to make sure the final product is the best available. The research material consisting of legal decisions, statutory provisions, leading cases, scholarly analysis, case books, form books, law review articles, seminar notes, law school notes, and many other bits of facts and information and suggestions about writing wills and planning estates is carefully preserved by the lawyer in his "probate book." The probate book is used when other wills are written by the lawyer, perhaps, with a few additions, deletions or changes to keep the book current. I was always very proud of my book. It was organized in such a way that I could prepare a will for a typical young married man by saying to my secretary—after the conference with the client—"type a will for Mr. Jones using paragraphs 1, 3, 7, 8, and 12." My secretary would select the legal size paper, put it into the machine and push a few buttons and, presto, a will emerges.

I don't mean to dramatize or oversimplify the will writing procedures by lawyers. I do mean to convey the idea that in 95 percent to 98 percent of the cases there are no significant problems and it is easy to prepare a will if you know what you are doing. The following procedures will enable over 90 percent of the American people to prepare their own wills.

First, however, let me explain what is meant by unusual or extraordinary problems and serious tax problems for those few (less than 5 percent) who should not do it themselves. An unusual or extraordinary problem which generally requires attention from a specialist includes such situations as the following:

1. Antenuptial Agreements: It is unusual for a person about to be married not to want his or her spouse to have a part of his or her estate. However, when this

does occur, it is generally motivated by tax considerations.

2. Incompetent dependents: This status frequently requires special arrangements and attention.

3. Bitter, hostile, divorce proceedings, court decrees, and property settlement agreements: These kinds of cases require a lawyer to handle the sticky situation more than the writing of a will after the problems are resolved, if ever.

4. Expectation of inheritance which may generate tax problems: We all hope for these situations, but if it should happen to you—get a lawyer!

5. Second marriages: Two or more marriages with free-floating anxiety and hostility involving former spouses and children from one or more prior marriages can cause more problems than most lawyers can solve.

In terms of writing wills and estate planning, serious tax problems generally denote an estate large enough to be taxable under the applicable estate tax code. Under the old code (before 1977) there was a $60,000 exemption for single persons and the marital deduction for married persons. Under the new tax laws the exemptions are now much higher. Thus, if you are single and have an estate in excess of $175,625 or married with over $525,625 you may have tax consequences in your estate planning and will writing. If you do you should consider the advisability of retaining a lawyer or other professional.

The Main Parts of a Will

We then reach the conclusion previously mentioned: based on probate records available, approximately 3 percent of the population in this nation have assets sufficient to generate a taxable estate under the new code. Under these circumstances almost everyone except the 3 percent can write his or her own will. Now for the procedures.

The usual provisions of a typical will include the following:

1. Introductory Clause to identify the testator
2. Special Instructions (if any)
3. Appointment of Fiduciaries
4. Specific Gifts
5. General Gifts
6. Residuary Clause
7. Trust for Minor Children
8. Marital Deduction Clause
9. Common Disaster Clause
10. Execution (signing)
11. Attestation and Signatures of Witnesses

Each of these parts with suggested language will be listed and discussed briefly. Alternative or additional clauses are also listed.

Introductory Clause

Immediately preceding the Introductory Clause is the title of the document which is usually as follows: LAST WILL AND TESTAMENT OF JOHN DOE.

The usual Introductory Clause which appears in most wills and in most archaic style form books:

I, JOHN DOE, domiciliary of, and a resident of, 111 First Street, City of Boulder, County of Boulder, and State of Colorado, being of sound and disposing mind and memory and hereby intending to dispose of all property belonging to me at my death, of whatever kind and wherever situate, do make, publish and declare this to be my Last Will and Testament, and hereby revoke all former wills and codicils by me made.

Modern Style:

I, JOHN DOE, of Boulder, Colorado, make this my will and revoke my prior wills and codicils.

The essential function of this part of the will is to identify the testator and to express an intention to make a will.

Special Instructions

This part is not necessary and it is frequently recommended that it be omitted entirely. It is not necessary to direct the payment of debts because the law requires it.

It can include:

I direct that I be buried on my family's plot in _____ _____ .

I direct that my body shall be cremated after my death.

Appointment of Fiduciaries

 Executor—Executrix

I appoint my wife, Jane Doe, Executrix of this, my Last Will. If my wife shall fail to qualify or having qualified, shall die, resign, or cease to act as Executrix, then I appoint my son, Tom Doe, as executor in her place and stead. In case of the death, incapacity, or refusal to act of both, I appoint The First National Bank and Trust Company of _____ as Executor.

Trustee

I appoint my brother, Tim Doe, Trustee under this my will. If my brother shall fail to qualify, or having qualified, shall die, resign or cease to act for any reason, I appoint my sister, Kim Doe, in place of my brother. If my sister shall fail to qualify, or having qualified, shall die, resign, or cease to act for any reason, I appoint such person as my brother shall designate, by instrument in writing duly acknowledged, as his substitute or successor. If my brother shall fail to make such designation, then I appoint The First National Bank of _____ as Trustee.

Guardian

If my spouse should not survive me, I name _____ _____ of the City of _____ Guardian of the person of any of my children during their minority. If he/she fails to act or ceases to act as Guardian, I name _____ _____ and his/her wife/husband _____ , or the survivor of them if one is deceased, as Guardians of the person of any of my children who are minors at the time.

Special Gifts

I give all of the shares of the common stock of Doe Corporation or any successor thereto by merger, consolidation, or otherwise which I may own at the time of my death to my son, Tom Doe, if he shall survive me.

I give my five carat, round, solitare diamond ring with two baguettes to my daughter, Linda Doe, if she shall survive me.

I give all my law books, office equipment, and all property contained in my law office to my son, Tom Doe, if he shall survive me.

I give all of the real property owned by me at Vail, Colorado, together with all improvements thereon, all appurtenances thereto, and all unexpired policies of fire, liability and other insurance relating to said premises and any claims I may have at the time of my death on any such policies of insurance, to my wife Jane, if she shall survive me.

General Gifts

I give the sum of Five Thousand Dollars ($5,000) to my brother, Tim Doe, if he shall survive me.

Residuary Clause

I give the residue of my estate to my wife, Jane, if she survives me. If my wife, Jane, predeceases me, I give said property in equal shares, to my three children, Tom, Linda, and Ann.

Trust for Minor Children

The share of any legatee who shall be under the age of 18 (21, 25) years, shall not be paid to such legatee but shall instead be held in trust to apply to his or her use all the income thereof, and also such amounts of the principal, even to the extent of all, as my Trustee deems necessary or suitable for the support, welfare, and education of such legatees; and when he or she attains the age of 18 (21, 25) years to pay him or her the remaining principal, if any. If any legatee for whom a share is held in trust should die before having received all the principal thereof, then upon his or her death the remaining principal shall be paid to his or her then living child or children, equally if more than one, and in default thereof, to my then living descendants, per stirpes.

Common Disaster Clause

Under ordinary circumstances, it is expensive and illogical for property to pass through successive estates where the testator and a legatee die within a very short time of each other. Therefore, it is good practice for the testator to be deemed to survive, in the event of a common disaster, for purposes of distribution under his will.

Usual Common Disaster Clause is:

If any beneficiary and I should die in a common accident or disaster or under such circumstances that it is doubtful who died first, (or within 30, 60, 90, days of my death), then all the provisions of this will shall take effect as if such beneficiary had in fact predeceased me.

Another form:

If my wife should die at the same time as I, or within (10, 30, 60, 90) days after my death, then I give and bequeath my estate to _____ .

Execution

IN WITNESS WHEREOF, I have hereunto set my hand and seal this _____ day of _____ , 19__.

_____
John Doe

Attestation and Signature of Witnesses

The foregoing instrument, consisting of two (2) typewritten pages, including this page, was signed, sealed, published, and declared by the said John Doe as his Last Will and Testament, in the presence of each of us, who at his request and in his presence and in the presence of one another, subscribe our names hereto as witnesses on the day of the date hereof; and we declare that at the time of the execution of this instrument the said John Doe, according to our best knowledge and belief, was of sound and disposing mind and memory and under no constraint.

_____ residing at _____

_____ residing at _____

_____ residing at _____

Self Proof of Will

State of _____

County of _____

We, _____ , _____ , and __

_____ , the testator and the witnesses respectively, whose names are signed to the attached or foregoing instrument, were sworn and declared to the undersigned officer that the testator signed the instrument as his last will, that he signed, and that each of the witnesses, in the presence of the testator and in the presence of each other, signed the will as a witness.

_____

Testator

_____

Witness

_____

Witness

_____

Witness

Subscribed and sworn to before me by _____

_____ , the testator, and by _____ , _____

_____ , and _____ , the witnesses

on the ____ day of _____ , 19 __ .

_____

Official Capacity of Officer

Checklist for Preparation of Your Own Will

The final step in being able to draft a will is to assemble all of the facts and information about your estate, family, and personal situation. This is very important because it clearly defines your personal situation and enables you to answer questions. The following checklist is designed to assist you in collecting the facts you need. As you compile the information and identify each item that should be covered in the will, you can turn to the forms and draft an appropriate provision to resolve the question.

1. Name of Testator (your name)
   a. Are you known by any other name?
   b. Have you used other names in the past?
   c. If a name change has occurred, are the legal papers in order?

2. Domicile
   a. Do you own or maintain a residence outside the state in which the will is to be executed?
   b. Should a definitive statement be made in the will as to your intent regarding domicile or residence?

3. Age
   a. Do the dates on birth certificate and insurance policies coincide?
   b. Is evidence of your birthdate sufficient for social security purposes?

4. Family
   a. Are you married, single, a widow, widower, or adopted?

b. Any previous marriages?

c. What are the names, address, ages, and marital status of your children?

d. Are there any adopted children?

e. Are there any deceased children?

f. Do you intend to disinherit any of your children?

g. Are any provisions to be made for children born after your death?

h. Are any provisions to be made for individuals who may claim to be your children?

i. Have advances been made to any of the children?

j. If so, are they to be deducted from the gifts to the children?

k. Are your parents living?

l. Do you want to provide for them?

m. Do you want to provide for any grandchildren?

n. Do you want to provide for any other relatives?

5. Guardian

a. Do you want a guardian to be appointed for your (infant) children?

b. If so, who shall be appointed?

c. Is guardian to be required to give bond?

d. What provision should be made for the support of your children?

6. Funeral Instructions

a. Do you have a preference as to how your body should be disposed of?

b. Are any provisions regarding cemetery lot, tombstone, and upkeep of the cemetery lot to be provided for in the will?

7. Prior Wills and Codicils

   a. Do you have copies of prior wills and codicils?

   b. Are all prior wills and codicils to be revoked?

   c. Have you made provisions to destroy any prior wills?

8. Debts

   a. Do you have any existing debts?

   b. Do you have any liability, such as surety on a bond, pledge to any charity, or the like?

   c. Are debts to be paid from any specific property?

   d. What property is mortgaged or has other liens?

   e. Is mortgage or lien to be paid by the person or persons who receive your property, from the general estate or from a particular fund?

   f. What property is to be sold first to pay any debts of the estate?

   g. If a gift is made to a creditor, is it to be in payment of your indebtedness or an addition thereto?

9. Debts Owned to You

   a. Are any debts to be canceled?

   b. Are special provisions to be made for their payment?

   c. If a legacy is given to one who is indebted to you, is the debt to be deducted from that legacy?

10. Husband and Wife

   a. Was an antenuptial agreement ever made?

   b. Are gifts to be in lieu of dower or curtesy?

   c. Are gifts to stop if the surviving spouse remarries?

   d. Are the family living expenses to be provided during the period of time when the estate is being settled?

   e. Is property to be given to your spouse in fee simple absolute (a fee without any condition or limitation whatsoever) or a life interest (interest held only during the term of a person's life)?

11. Property Owned by You

   a. Is there any property in your name that belongs to someone else?

   b. What is to be done with your property which is held as an agent or trustee for another?

   c. What property is to be specifically bequeathed or devised and to whom?

   d. What is to be done with your business, if any?

   e. What property is held jointly?

   f. Have you created any living trust?

   g. Have you any future or contingent interest?

   h. If a gift is made to a class (a group such as the grandchildren, all nieces and nephews, etc.) and a member of the class dies, shall the survivors of the deceased member of the class receive that share or is it to be equally divided among the other members?

i. When are the members of the class determined?

j. Real property

    (1) What real property do you own?

    (2) Is the property owned in fee simple?

    (3) Has any real property been bought or sold on contract for deed?

    (4) Is any of this property mortgaged?

    (5) If mortgaged, is the devise to be subject to the mortgage?

    (6) Do you have a power of appointment to any real property?

    (7) Is there any real property located outside the state where you live?

    (8) What real property is to be specifically devised and to whom?

    (9) In whose name is the title to your family home?

    (10) Is gift to be in fee or for life?

    (11) If gift is for life, who is to be the remainder-man (the person who receives the remainder—property remaining after the death of the person who received the original life interest)?

k. Personal property

    (1) What specific items are to be bequeathed and to whom?

(2) What money legacies, if any, are to be made and to whom?

(3) How are personal effects to be disposed of?

(4) Are any particular proceeds of insurance payable to the estate to be disposed of?

(5) How are proceeds of insurance payable to the estate to be disposed of?

(6) If property is disposed of or consumed during your life, is the gift to fail, or is it to be made up in some other way?

l.   Residuary Clause

(1) What shall be done with the balance of estate after all bequests have been paid or devises of real estate made or trust set up and all debts paid?

m. Partnership Property

(1) Are you a member of any partnership?

(2) Are there articles of partnership?

(3) What provision is to be made as to the disposition of the interest of the partner and the partnership?

(4) Is there a separate buy and sell agreement?

12. Trusts

a.   Is any of your property to be left in trust?

b.   Who is to be the appointed trustee?

c.   What is to be done if the trustee dies, resigns, or is unable to act?

d. To whom is the income to be paid and how is the principal to be distributed?

e. What powers and duties are to be specifically imposed upon the trustee?

f. Is liability of the trustee to be specifically limited?

g. What is the duration of the trust?

h. Do you want to provide for a spend thrift beneficiary?

i. Can corpus (principal) of trust be invaded?

j. Is any special provision to be made as to compensation of the trustee or trustees?

13. Conditional Gifts

a. Are any gifts to be conditional?

b. Are any provisions to be made for disinheriting persons who may contest the will?

14. Charities

a. What gifts, if any, are to be given to charities?

15. Employees or Servants of You, the Testator

a. Are any gifts to be given to them?

16. Interest

a. When is the payment of legacies to be made?

b. Are any special provisions to be made as to payment of interest on legacies?

17. Taxes

a. Are inheritance taxes to be charged against each gift or paid out of the general estate?

b. Are provisions made to get maximum benefits of

the marital deduction clause?

18. Executor

    a. Who is to be the executor(s)?

    b. If more than one, is the majority to decide?

    c. Are provisions made if the executor decides or refuses to act as such?

    d. Will the executor be required to give bond?

    e. Are provisions made for the executor's compensation?

    f. What powers are to be given to the executor?

    g. What directions, if any, as to winding up or carrying on the business of the estate?

    h. Would you like your executor to confer with any friend or associate in connection with the estate?

    i. If so, is the will to name one or more of them as advisors to the executor?

FORM 2: Holographic Will

Last Will and Testament of _____

This is my last will. I revoke all prior Wills or Codicils. I give all of my property to my wife, _____ , appoint her Executrix of this will, and waive all bonds. If my wife, _____ , does not survive me, then I give all my property to my three children, _____ , _____ , and _____ , share and share alike, and I appoint my brother, _____ ____ , Executor, and waive all bonds.

This will is dated, written, and signed entirely by me in my own handwriting.

Dated this ____ day of _____ , 19__ .

(Signature)

FORM 3: Single Person: Estate to Parents

Last Will and Testament of _____

I, _____ , a resident of _____ , City of _____ , County of _____ , State of _____ , hereby make this Will, and revoke all prior Wills.

1. I direct that my debts and funeral expenses be paid by my Executor/ Executrix as soon as practicable after my death.

2. I give, devise, and bequeath my entire estate, real, personal or mixed, wherever situated, of which I may die seized or possessed, or to which I may be or become in any way entitled to have any interest, or over which I may have any power of appointment, to my mother, _____ , or, if she predeceases me, then to my father, _____ .

3. I hereby nominate and appoint _____ , Executor/ Executrix of this Will. I direct that no bond or other security shall be required of my Executor/Executrix for the faithful performance of his/her duties.

IN WITNESS WHEREOF I have subscribed and sealed and do publish and declare these presents as and for my Will in the presence of the witnesses attesting the same this ____ day of _____ , 19__ .

(Signature)

ATTESTATION AND WITNESSES

The foregoing instrument, consisting of ____ typewritten pages, including this page, was signed, sealed, published, and declared by the said _____ as his/her Last Will and Testament, in the presence of each of us, who at his/her request and in his/her presence and in the presence of one another, subscribe our names hereto as witnesses on the day of the date hereof; and we declare at the time of the execution of this instrument the said _____ , according to our best knowledge and belief, was of sound and disposing mind and memory and under no constraint.

_____ residing at _____

_____

_____ residing at _____

_____ residing at _____

FORM 4: Widow or Widower: Estate to Children

Last Will and Testament of _____

I, _____ , a resident of and domiciled in the City of _____ , County of _____ , State of _____ , do make, publish, and declare this to be my Last Will and Testament, hereby revoking all Wills and Codicils heretofore made by me.

1. I direct that my debts and funeral expenses be paid by my Executor as soon as practicable after my death.

2. I give and bequeath the sum of _____ to my son, _____ , if he shall survive me.

3. I give and bequeath the sum of _____ to my daughter, _____ _____ , if she shall survive me.

4. All the rest, residue, and remainder of my estate, real, personal and mixed, and wheresoever situated, I give, devise, and bequeath to my children share and share alike per stirpes.

5. I hereby appoint my son, _____ , Executor hereunder and if he predeceases me, fails to qualify, or ceases to act, I appoint my daughter, _____ , Executrix hereunder. No Executor or Executrix named herein shall be required to give bond for the faithful performance of their duties hereunder.

IN WITNESS WHEREOF I have hereunto set my hand this ___ day of _____ , 19__ .

(Signature)

[Attestation, Witnesses, and Self Proof of Will should be attached.]

FORM 5: Married Person: Entire Estate to Spouse or Alternatively to Children

Last Will and Testament of _____

I, _____ , of _____ , City of _____ , County of _____ , State of _____ , being of sound mind and memory, do hereby revoke any and all Wills and Codicils heretofore made by me, and do make, publish, and declare this to be my Last Will and Testament.

1. I direct that all my just debts, funeral expenses, and costs of administration be paid out of the principal of my estate.

2. I give, devise, and bequeath to my wife/husband, _____ , all of the property of all kinds, wherever situated, belonging to me at the time of my death, to be hers/his absolutely. As I make this bequest, I have my children, _____ , _____ , and _____ _____ , in my mind, and I feel that I have made adequate provision for them before the execution of this Will. I have in mind, also, that my wife/husband will take care and provide for them in the manner we both desire.

3. I hereby nominate and appoint my wife/husband, _____ , Executrix/Executor of this Will. In the event of her/his death, or refusal or inability to act, I hereby nominate and appoint my brother, _____ _____ , to act as successor Executor, with all the rights and duties herein given to or imposed upon my Executrix/Executor. I direct that neither of them shall be required to furnish bond.

4. In the event that my wife/husband, _____ , shall die with me in a common accident or disaster, or under such circumstances as may make it impossible or difficult to determine which of us died first, or within sixty (60) days after my death, I direct that my wife/husband shall be conclusively deemed not to have survived me.

5. In the event that my wife/husband, _____ , shall predecease me or shall be deemed not to have survived me in accordance with the provisions of Paragraph "4," all of the property of all kinds, wherever situated, belonging to me at the time of my death, I give, devise, and bequeath to my brother, _____ , whom I hereby nomi-

nate and appoint as Trustee, to be held in Trust upon the terms and conditions hereinafter provided:

a. Until my beloved daughter, _____ , shall attain the age of twenty-one (21) years, the Trustee shall pay to her or for her benefit, from the income or principal of the Trust, such sum or sums as the Trustee shall deem necessary or proper to provide for her suitable support, education, and maintenance, adding any unused income to the principal at the end of each year.

b. When _____ shall attain the age of twenty-one (21) years, the Trustee shall distribute to her one-third of the principal of the Trust. The Trustee shall thereafter continue to pay to her or for her benefit, from the income or principal of the Trust, such sum or sums as the Trustee shall deem necessary or proper to provide for her suitable support, education, and maintenance, adding any unused income to the principal at the end of each year. If and when she shall attain the age of thirty (30) years, the Trustee is directed to distribute to her or for her benefit, from the income or principal of the Trust, such sums as the Trustee shall deem necessary or proper to provide for her suitable support, and maintenance, adding any unused income to the principal at the end of each year. When she shall attain the age of thirty-five (35) years, the Trustee is directed to distribute to her the remaining principal and all accumulated income of the Trust.

c. In the event of the death of _____ prior to the termination of this Trust, then the Trustee shall distribute the principal of the Trust, to her then living children, and if none shall then be living, then the principal of the Trust shall be distributed to my other children, or their issue, per stirpes.

d. If any portion of the principal of the Trust shall be payable to a beneficiary who is then less than twenty-one (21) years of age, such portion shall immediately vest in such beneficiary, but distribution thereof shall be postponed by the Trustee until such beneficiary attains the age of twenty-one (21) years, and in the meantime, the Trustee shall pay such part of the income on such portion, and the principal thereof, as the Trustee shall deem necessary or proper to provide for such beneficiary's suitable support, education, and maintenance, adding any unused income to the principal at the end of each year.

106

e. Whenever and as often as any beneficiary of the Trust to whom payments are herein directed to be made shall be under a legal disability, or, in the sole judgment of the Trustee, shall otherwise be unable to apply such payments to his or her own best interest and advantage, the Trustee may make all or any portion of such payments by expending the same for the benefit of the beneficiary, or by making payments to the legal guardian or conservator of such beneficiary, or to a relative of such beneficiary to be expended for the beneficiary's benefit; and the decision of the Trustee in each such case shall be binding upon all beneficiaries hereunder.

f. No person dealing with the Trustee shall be obliged to inquire as to his powers or to see to the application of any money or property delivered to him. The Trustee shall not be required to obtain authority or approval of any court in the exercise of any power conferred upon him hereunder. The Trustee shall not be required to furnish a bond for the proper performance of his duties hereunder.

g. If the Trustee shall be compelled at any time during the existence of this Trust, or thereafter, to pay any tax, or penalty, or interest with respect thereto for any reason, he shall be entitled to be reimbursed from the principal of the Trust; or if the Trust principal be then insufficient, or if it be then terminated the Trustee shall be reimbursed by the persons to whom the principal of the Trust shall have been distributed to the extent of the amount received by each distributee. The Trustee, before making any distribution of either income or principal, may accordingly require an undertaking in form satisfactory to the Trustee to reimburse him, or he may withhold distribution pending determination or release of any tax lien.

h. The Trustee may resign and appoint a successor Trustee by giving ten days written notice to each income beneficiary. If for any reason there is at any time no Trustee acting hereunder, I hereby nominate and appoint _____ Trust Company, successor Trustee, with all the rights and duties herein given to or imposed upon my Trustee.

6. No disposition, charge, or encumbrance of either the income or principal of the Trust, or of any part thereof, by my daughter, _____ , by way of anticipation, shall be of any validity or legal effect, or be in any wise regarded by the Trustee and no such income

107

or principal, or any part thereof, shall in any wise be liable to any claim of any creditor of such beneficiary.

7. In the investment, administration, and distribution of my estate and of the Trust hereby created and of the several shares thereof (except where otherwise restricted), the Executrix/Executor and the Trustee may perform every act in the management of my estate or of the Trust which individuals may perform in the management of like property owned by them free of any trust, without authorization of any court, even though any such act would not be authorized or appropriate for fiduciaries (but for this power) under any statutory or other rule of law, including in this grant power: to acquire by purchase or otherwise and to retain, temporarily or permanently, any and all kinds of realty and personalty, even common stocks and unsecured obligations, without diversification as to kind or amount; to sell or otherwise dispose of any such property, publicly or privately, wholly or partly on credit; to delegate discretion; and to distribute in kind or in money, or partly in each, even if shares be composed differently.

8. In the event my wife/husband, _____ , shall not survive me, or shall die with me in a common accident or disaster, or within sixty (60) days after my death, I hereby appoint my sister, _____ , City of _____ , State of _____ , as Guardian of the person of my daughter, _____ .

IN WITNESS WHEREOF I have set my hand to this Last Will and Testament, and on the margin of each page of which I have affixed my signature for better identification, this ____ day of _____ , 19__ .

(Signature)

[Attestation, Witnesses, and Self Proof of Will should be attached.]

Alternative Clauses

There may be some additional objectives you will want to accomplish in your will. The following additional clauses are selected to cover these situations.

Inclusion of Adopted Children

Whenever the word "child" or "children" is used in this will, it shall include lawfully adopted child or children of mine.

Exclusion of Adopted Children

The words "child," "children," "issue," and any other word used herein to indicate descendants shall be construed to exclude children by adoption.

Bequest of Automobile

I give unto my wife, Jane, if she shall survive me, any automobile or automobiles which I shall own at the time of my death. In the event my wife shall not survive me, then such automobile or automobiles shall be and become a part of my residuary estate.

Bequest of Household Goods

I hereby give to my wife, Jane, all of the household goods, furnishings, and equipment located in and used by me in my home at _____ , or which at the time of my death may be located in the premises which I then occupy as my homestead.

Devise of Family Home

If I own a house and plot of ground at the time of my death, which is being used by me and my wife as a family home, then I give such house and plot of ground unto my wife, subject, however, to any encumbrances thereon existing at the time of my death (or free from any encumbrance thereon at the time of my death).

Appointment of Executor/Executrix

I hereby appoint _____ and _____ _____ Executors/Executrixes of this my Last Will and Testament.

I do hereby appoint _____ to be the Executor/Executrix of this my Last Will and Testament, and I request that he/she be not required to give bond for the performance of the duties of such office.

I nominate and appoint _____ of _____ County, State of _____ , to be Executor/Executrix of this my Last Will and Testament. In case of his/her death during my life or of his/her incapacity or refusal to act, I nominate and appoint _____ of _____ , _____ County, _____ , as such Executor/Executrix. In case of the death, incapacity, or refusal to act of both said _____ and said _____ ____ , I nominate and appoint _____ as such Executor/Executrix.

Appointment of Guardian

I hereby appoint my sister, _____ , as Guardian of the person of my infant children, _____ _____ and _____ , during the minority of each.

I do hereby appoint _____ as Guardian of the person of my minor children, _____ and _____ , during that time each of such children is a minor.

If my spouse should not survive me, I name _____ _____ , of _____ , City of _____ , County of __ ____ , State of _____ , Guardian of the person of any of my children during their minority. If he/she fails or ceases to act as Guardian, I name _____ , and his/her wife/husband _____ , both of _____ , City of _____ , County of _____ , State

110

of _____ , or the survivor of them if one is deceased, as Guardians or Guardian of the person of any of my children who are minors at the time. I name the _____ _____ Bank as Guardian of the estates of any of my children who are minors at the time.

Specific Devises

I give, devise, and bequeath to my wife, _____ ___ , if she survives me, in fee simple, the buildings and land located at _____ , City of _____ , State of _____ . If my wife does not survive me, this gift shall lapse and the property described herein shall fall into and become part of my residuary estate.

I give and devise to my wife, _____ , if she survives me, or if not, in equal shares to my children who survive me, their heirs and assigns forever, all real estate owned by me at the time of my death, including all buildings and improvements thereon, and the rights and other interests pertaining thereto.

I give and devise to my son, _____ , and my daughter, _____ , share and share alike, per stirpes and not per capita, the real property owned by me at _____ , County of _____ , State of _____ , and further described as follows:
[Legal Description here]

Specific Legacies

I give and bequeath to my wife, _____ , if she survives me, all my furniture, furnishings, books, linens, silver, china, glassware, jewelry, wearing apparel, automobiles, and all other household and personal goods and effects.

To my daughter, _____ , I give my diamond ring and my gold watch. If my daughter does not survive me, this legacy shall lapse and become part of my residuary estate.

111

I give and bequeath all my law books, office equipment, and all property contained in my law office to my son, _____ , if he shall survive me.

Spendthrift Trust

The income reserved to the respective beneficiaries of any trust created by this will shall not be subject to anticipation, or to pledge, assignment, sale, or transfers in any manner to charge or encumber such interest, nor shall such interest be liable or subject in any manner while in the possession of the trustee for the liabilities of any beneficiary, whether such liabilities arise from his debts, contracts, torts, or other engagements of any type.

No principal or income payable, or to become payable, in any trust created by this will shall be subject to anticipation or assignment by any beneficiary thereof, or to attachment by or to the interference of control of any creditor of any such beneficiary, as to be taken or reached by any legal or equitable process in satisfaction of any debt or liability of such beneficiary, prior to its actual receipt by the beneficiary.

I direct that all legacies and devises and all shares and interests in my estate, whether principal or income, while in the hands of my executor or trustees, shall not be anticipated, alienated, or in any other manner assigned or transferred by the legatee, devises, or beneficiaries, and shall be free and exempt from anticipation, execution, assignment, pledge, attachment, distress for rent, and other legal or equitable process which may be instituted by and on behalf of, any creditor or assignee of such legatee, devisee, or beneficiary, or his or her spouse.

Common Disaster Clauses

If any person dies with me in a common disaster, and if such person is required to survive me in order to take property under this will, then such property shall vest as if such person had predeceased me.

112

If my wife and I shall die simultaneously or under circumstances which make it difficult to determine which of us died first, I direct that my wife shall be deemed to have survived me for the purposes of this will, and I direct further that the provisions of this will shall be construed upon the assumption irrespective of any provisions of law establishing a contrary presumption or requiring survivorship for a fixed period as a condition of taking property by inheritance.

Omission of Certain Persons

I give, devise, and bequeath to _____ , daughter of _____ , nothing, for the reason that I have heretofore given her a sum of money out of my estate equal in amount to her share as compared with her brother and sisters, and I will therefore give her no more.

Omission of Certain Relatives

I have made no provision in this my will for my brothers and sister, or her son, because they are already amply provided for.

Bequest of Business

I give and bequeath the goodwill and benefit of the business of _____ , which I am now carrying on at _____ , and all of my capital and property which shall be employed therein at my decease and also the leaseheld premises situated at _____ , wherein said business is now being carried on, for all my term and interest therein, unto my son, _____ , absolutely.

Bequest of Unpublished Manuscripts

To _____ , all unpublished manuscripts, to be handled by her/him in accordance with instructions which I have given.

7

Statutory Provisions of all Fifty States

You can learn about wills, but if you do not comply with the mandatory requirements of your state statutes in executing the document, you won't have a valid, legal will. In fact, it is not a "will" unless it complies with the requirements of the statutes of your state, or the state in which it was written.

Under these circumstances I have made a special effort in writing this book to give you the essential facts and information you need to write your own will—how to use the right words or phrases to accomplish your objectives to legally execute (sign) it and have it properly witnessed (attested) in accordance with the laws of your own state. Now that you know how to write your own will you need to know more about the specific requirements of the statutes of your state regarding the signing and witnessing. This chapter contains a summary review of the essential parts of all 50 state statutes governing wills. The items covered show you (1) who may make a will, (2) how many witnesses are required, (3) holographic will provisions, if any, (4) nuncupative will provisions, if any, and (5) revocation (cancellation) of wills.

It is a fundamental principle of law in all states that a person must be of sound mind to write a will, and there are, of course, certain contingencies which may void a will. For example, fraud, mistake, undue influence, etc. Moreover, some changes in your family situation such as marriage, divorce, annulment, subsequent birth of children, adoption of children, or other matters may change the effect of a will. To revoke a will there must be an intent to revoke. A written revocation executed in accordance with your state statutes is effective to revoke a will in all states. You should be alert to all these factors in your overall estate planning and in your review of your estate plans and wills.

Knowing how to write your will, how to execute it, and having it witnessed—all in accordance with the governing laws—will be easy for you after you study the material in this book and review the requirements of your state statutes.

Alabama
1. Who May Make a Will:
   a. Realty: Every person of the age of nineteen.
   b. Personal Property: All persons over the age of 18.
2. Witnesses: Two.
3. Holographic Wills: No provision.
4. Nuncupative Wills: $500 or less (43-1-31).
5. Revocation: Burned, torn, canceled, or obliterated.

Alaska

1. Who May Make a Will: Any person 18 or more years of age.

2. Witnesses: Two.

3. Holographic Wills: A will is valid as a holographic will if the signature and the material provision are in the handwriting of the testator.

4. Nuncupative Wills: Under the Alaska statutes nuncupative wills are limited to mariners and soldiers.

5. Revocation: Burned, torn, canceled, obliterated, or destroyed.

Arizona

1. Who May Make a Will: Any person 18 or more years of age.

2. Witnesses: Two.

3. Holographic Wills: A will which does not comply with Section 14-2502 is valid as a holographic will, whether or not witnessed, if the signature and the material provisions are in the handwriting of the testator.

4. Nuncupative Wills: No provision.

5. Revocation: Burned, torn, canceled, obliterated, or destroyed.

Arkansas

1. Who May Make a Will: Any person of sound mind 18 years of age or older.

2. Witnesses: Two.

3. Holographic Wills: When the entire body of a will and signature are in the handwriting of the testator, it may be established by the evidence of at least three disinterested witnesses to the handwriting and signature of the testator, without subscribing witnesses.

4. Nuncupative Wills: No provision.

5. Revocation: Burned, torn, canceled, obliterated, or destroyed.

California

1. Who May Make a Will: Every person of sound mind, over the age of 18 years.

2. Witnesses: Two; must *sign at the end of the will.* Testator *must also sign at the end.*

3. Holographic Wills: A holographic will is one that is entirely written, dated, and signed by the hand of the testator himself. It is subject to no other form, and need not be witnessed. No address, date, or other matter written, printed, or stamped upon the document, which is not incorporated in the provisions which are in the handwriting of the decedent, shall be considered as any part of the will.

4. Nuncupative Wills: A nuncupative will may dispose of personal property only, and the estate bequeathed must not exceed one thousand dollars in value.

5. Revocation: Burned, torn, canceled, defaced, obliter-

ated, or destroyed; by duress, menace, fraud, or undue influence; by marriage or after born children.

Colorado

1. Who May Make a Will: Any person 18 years of age or older.
2. Witnesses: Two.
3. Holographic Wills: A will which does not comply with Section 15-11-502 is valid as a holographic will, whether or not witnesses, if the signature and the material provisions are in the handwriting of the testator.
4. Nuncupative Wills: No provision.
5. Revocation: Burned, torn, canceled, obliterated, or destroyed.

Connecticut

1. Who May Make a Will: Any person of the age of 18 years.
2. Witnesses: Two.
3. Holographic Wills: No provision.
4. Nuncupative Wills: No provision.
5. Revocation: Burned, canceled, torn or obliterated.

Delaware

1. Who May Make a Will: Any person of the age of 18 years.

2. Witnesses: Two.

3. Holographic Wills: No provision.

4. Nuncupative Wills: No provision.

5. Revocation: Canceled.

District of Columbia

1. Who May Make a Will: 18 years of age.

2. Witnesses: Two.

3. Holographic Wills: No provision.

4. Nuncupative Wills: Nuncupative wills are invalid, except when made by soldiers in active service or mariners at sea, during their last sickness. If reduced to writing within ten days, and if proved by two witnesses requested to act as such by the testator, such wills may dispose of personalty.

5. Revocation: Burned, canceled, torn, or obliterated.

Florida

1. Who May Make a Will: Any person 18 years of age.

2. Witnesses: Two.

3. Holographic Wills: No provision.

4. Nuncupative Wills: No provision.

5. Revocation: Burned, torn, canceled, defaced, obliterated, or destroyed.

Georgia

1. Who May Make a Will: Infants under 14 years of age

are considered wanting in that discretion necessary to make a will.

2. Witnesses: Two.
3. Holographic Wills: No provision.
4. Nuncupative Wills: 113-501, 504.
5. Revocation: Destroyed or obliterated.

Hawaii

1. Who May Make a Will: Any person 18 or more years of age.
2. Witnesses: Two.
3. Holographic Wills: No provision.
4. Nuncupative Wills: No provision.
5. Revocation: Burned, torn, canceled, obliterated, or destroyed.

Idaho

1. Who May Make a Will: Any emancipated minor or any person 18 or more years of age.
2. Witnesses: Two.
3. Holographic Wills: A will which does not comply with Section 15-2-502 of this Part is valid as a holographic will, whether or not witnessed, if the signature and the material provisions are in the handwriting of the testator.
4. Nuncupative Wills: No provision.
5. Revocation: Burned, torn, canceled, obliterated, or destroyed.

Illinois

1. Who May Make a Will: Every person who has attained the age of 18.
2. Witnesses: Two.
3. Holographic Wills: No provision.
4. Nuncupative Wills: No provision.
5. Revocation: Burned, canceled, torn, or obliterated.

Indiana

1. Who May Make a Will: Any person of sound mind, who is 18 years of age or older, or who is younger and a member of the armed forces, or merchant marines may make a will.
2. Witnesses: Two.
3. Holographic Wills: No provision.
4. Nuncupative Wills: 29-1-5-6.
5. Revocation: Destroyed or mutilated.

Iowa

1. Who May Make a Will: Any person of full age.
2. Witnesses: Two.
3. Holographic Wills: No provision.
4. Nuncupative Wills: No provision.
5. Revocation: Canceled or destroyed.

Kansas

1. Who May Make a Will: Any person of sound mind and possessing rights of majority.

2. Witnesses: Two.

3. Holographic Wills: No provision.

4. Nuncupative Wills: A nuncupative will made in the last sickness of the testator is valid in respect to personal property if the will is reduced to writing and subscribed by two disinterested witnesses within 30 days after the speaking of the testamentary words, when the testator called on some person present to bear testimony to said disposition as his will.

5. Revocation: Burned, torn, canceled, obliterated, or destroyed.

Kentucky

1. Who May Make a Will: Every person of sound mind and 18 years of age.

2. Witnesses: Two.

3. Holographic Wills: No provision.

4. Nuncupative Wills: No provision.

5. Revocation: Cut, torn, burned, obliterated, canceled, or destroyed.

Louisiana

1. Who May Make a Will: One must be of sound mind to make a will, but it is sufficient if the will be made during lucid moment. (CC 1475)

2. Witnesses: The following persons are incapable of being witnesses to wills:

a. Persons under the age of sixteen;

b. Insane, deaf, dumb, or blind persons;

c. Persons whom the criminal laws declare incapable of exercising civil functions;

d. Married women to the wills of their husbands. There are also limitations on heirs or named legatees.

3. There are four classes of wills in Louisiana:

a. Nuncupative or open testaments;

b. Mystic or sealed testaments;

c. Olographic testaments; and

d. Statutory testaments. (CC 1574)

4. Revocation: Revocation of wills must be in one of the forms prescribed for testament or by intentional destruction of the will by the testator. (See Chapter 4.)

Maine

1. Who May Make a Will: A person of sound mind and of the age of 18 years.

2. Witnesses: Three.

3. Holographic Wills: No provision.

4. Nuncupative Wills: 18-51, 52, 53.

5. Revocation: Burned, canceled, torn, or obliterated.

Maryland

1. Who May Make a Will: Any person may make a will if he is 18 years of age or older.

2. Witnesses: Two.

3. Holographic Wills: 4-103.
4. Nuncupative Wills: No provision.
5. Revocation: Burned, canceled, torn, or obliterated.

Massachusetts
1. Who May Make a Will: A person 18 years or more.
2. Witnesses: Two.
3. Holographic Wills: No provision.
4. Nuncupative Wills: A soldier in actual service and a mariner at sea may dispose of his personal property by a nuncupative will.
5. Revocation: Burned, torn, canceled, or obliterated.

Michigan
1. Who May Make a Will: Any person of sound mind and who has attained the age of 18 years.
2. Witnesses: Two.
3. Holographic Wills: No provision.
4. Nuncupative Wills: Nuncupative wills proved by two competent witnesses are valid to dispose of an estate not exceeding $300; nuncupative wills of soldiers in actual military service and marines on shipboard are valid to dispose of their wages and personal estate.
5. Revocation: Burned, torn, canceled, or obliterated.

Minnesota
1. Who May Make a Will: Any person 18 years or more.

2. Witnesses: Two.
3. Holographic Wills: No provision.
4. Nuncupative Wills: No provision.
5. Revocation: Burned, torn, canceled, obliterated, or destroyed.

Mississippi
1. Who May Make a Will: Every person 18 years of age or older.
2. Witnesses: Two.
3. Holographic Wills: Holographic wills are valid if wholly written and subscribed by the testator himself or herself.
4. Nuncupative Wills: 91-5-15.
5. Revocation: Destroyed, canceled, or obliterated.

Missouri
1. Who May Make a Will: Any person 18 years of age or older.
2. Witnesses: Two.
3. Holographic Wills: No provision.
4. Nuncupative Wills: A nuncupative will is valid only if made in imminent peril of death and death resulted therefrom, declared to be his will before two disinterested witnesses, reduced to writing by or under the direction of a witness within 30 days, and submitted for probate within six months after death. It can dis-

pose only of personal property of not more than $500, and neither revokes or changes an existing written will. (474.340)

5. Revocation: Burned, canceled, torn, or obliterated.

Montana

1. Who May Make a Will: Any person 18 or more years of age.
2. Witnesses: Two.
3. Holographic Wills: A will which does not comply with Section 91A-2-502 is valid as a holographic will, whether or not witnessed, if the signature and material provisions are in the handwriting of the testator.
4. Nuncupative Wills: No provision.
5. Revocation: Burned, torn, canceled, obliterated, or destroyed.

Nebraska

1. Who May Make a Will: Any adult and any person 18 or more years of age.
2. Witnesses: Two.
3. Holographic Wills: A will which does not comply with Section 30-2327 is valid as a holographic will whether or not witnessed, if it is dated and if the signature and the material provisions are in the handwriting of the testator.
4. Nuncupative Wills: No provision.

5. Revocation: Burned, torn, canceled, obliterated, or destroyed.

Nevada
1. Who May Make a Will: Every person of sound mind, over the age of 18 years.
2. Witnesses: Two.
3. Holographic Wills:
   a. A holographic will is one that is entirely written, dated, and signed by the hand of the testator himself. It is subject to no other form, and may be made in or out of this state and need not be witnessed.
   b. Every person of sound mind, over the age of 18 years, including married women, may, by last holographic will, dispose of all of his or her estate, real or personal, the same being chargeable with the payment of the testator's debts.
   c. Such will shall be valid and have full effect for the purpose for which they are intended.
4. Nuncupative Wills:
   a. No nuncupative or verbal will shall be good unless:
      (1) The same be proved by two witnesses who were present at the making thereof; and
      (2) It be proved that the testator, at the time of pronouncing the same, did bid someone present to bear witness that such was his will, or word of like import; and

      (3) It was made at the time of the last sickness of the deceased.

    b. No nuncupative or verbal will shall be good where the estate bequeathed exceeds the value of $1,000.

5. Revocation: Burned, torn, canceled, or obliterated.

New Hampshire

1. Who May Make a Will: Every person of sane mind, of the age of 18 years or married although under that age, may dispose of all his or her property by will.
2. Witnesses: Three.
3. Holographic Wills: No provision.
4. Nuncupative Wills: 551-15.
5. Revocation: Canceled, torn, obliterated, or otherwise destroyed.

New Jersey

1. Who May Make a Will: Age 21.
2. Witnesses: Two.
3. Holographic Wills: No provision.
4. Nuncupative Wills: No provision.
5. Revocation: Burned, canceled, torn, or obliterated.

New Mexico

1. Who May Make a Will: Any person who has reached the age of majority.
2. Witnesses: Two.

3. Holographic Wills: No provision.
4. Nuncupative Wills: No provision.
5. Revocation: Burned, torn, canceled, obliterated, or destroyed.

New York

1. Who May Make a Will: Every person 18 years of age or over.
2. Witnesses: Two.
3. Holographic Wills; and
4. Nuncupative Wills: A will is *nuncupative* when it is unwritten, and the making thereof by the testator and its provisions are clearly established by at least two witnesses. A will is *holographic* when it is written entirely in the handwriting of the testator, and is not executed and attested in accordance with the formalities prescribed by 3-2.1. A nuncupative or holographic will is valid only if made by
   a. a member of the armed forces of the United States while in actual military service during a war, declared or undeclared, or other armed conflict in which members of the armed forces are engaged.
   b. a person who serves with or accompanies an armed force engaged in actual military or naval service during such war or other armed conflict, or
   c. a mariner while at sea.
5. Revocation: Burned, torn, cut, canceled, obliterated, or destroyed.

North Carolina

1. Who May Make a Will: Any person of sound mind, and 18 years of age or over.
2. Witnesses: Two.
3. Holographic Wills: 31-3.4.
4. Nuncupative Wills: A nuncupative will is a will made orally by a person who is in his last sickness or in imminent peril, and declared to be his will before two competent witnesses simultaneously present at the making thereof and especially requested by him to bear witness thereto.
5. Revocation: Burned, torn, canceled, obliterated, or destroyed.

North Dakota

1. Who May Make a Will: Any adult who is of sound mind may make a will.
2. Witnesses: Two.
3. Holographic Wills: A will which does not comply with Section 30.1-08-02 is valid as a holographic will, whether or not witnessed, if the signature and the material provisions are in the handwriting of the testator.
4. Nuncupative Wills: No provision.
5. Revocation: Burned, torn, canceled, obliterated, or destroyed.

Ohio

1. Who May Make a Will: Any person of 18 years or over, of sound mind and memory and not under restraint may make a will.
2. Witnesses: Two.
3. Holographic Wills: No provision.
4. Nuncupative Wills: Oral will made in the last sickness is valid as to personal estate if reduced to writing and subscribed by two competent disinterested witnesses within ten days after speaking of testamentary words, and if testator was of sound mind and memory and not under any restraint, and if he called upon some person present to bear testimony to said disposition as his will. Such will must be offered for probate within six months after testator's death. Oral will is void if a beneficiary is a witness.
5. Revocation: Torn, canceled, obliterated, or destroyed.

Oklahoma

1. Who May Make a Will: Every person over the age of 18, of sound mind, may, by last will, dispose of all his estate, real and personal.
2. Witnesses: Two.
3. Holographic Wills: A holographic will is one that is entirely written, dated and signed by the hand of the testator himself. It is subject to no other form, and may be made in or out of this state, and need not be witnessed.

4. Nuncupative Wills: 84-46.

5. Revocation: Burned, torn, canceled, or destroyed.

Oregon

1. Who May Make a Will: Any person who is 18 years of age or older or who has been lawfully married, and who is of sound mind, may make a will.

2. Witnesses: Two.

3. Holographic Wills: No provision.

4. Nuncupative Wills: No provision.

5. Revocation: Burned, torn, canceled, obliterated, or destroyed.

Pennsylvania

1. Who May Make a Will: Any person of sound mind 18 years of age or older may make a will.

2. Witnesses: Two.

3. Holographic Wills: No provision.

4. Nuncupative Wills: No provision.

5. Revocation: Burned, canceled, or obliterated.

Rhode Island

1. Who May Make a Will: Every person of sane mind and 18 years of age or upwards may by will dispose of all real and personal estate.

2. Witnesses: Two.

3. Holographic Wills; and Nuncupative Wills: Holographic wills and nuncupative wills are not recog-

nized, except that any soldier or airman in actual military service, or any mariner or seaman being at sea, may dispose of his personal estate as he might have done under common law.

4. Revocation: Burned, torn, or otherwise destroyed.

South Carolina

1. Who May Make a Will: Any person 18 years of age, of sound mind, may make a will.
2. Witnesses: Three.
3. Holographic Wills: No provision.
4. Nuncupative Wills: 21-7-60.
5. Revocation: Destroyed.

South Dakota

1. Who May Make a Will: Any person 18 or more years of age is of sound mind may make a will.
2. Witnesses: Two.
3. Holographic Wills: A will which does not comply with Section 29-2-6 is valid as a holographic will whether or not witnessed if it is dated and if the signature and the material provisions are in the handwriting of the testator.
4. Nuncupative Wills: No provision.
5. Revocation: Burned, torn, canceled, obliterated, or destroyed.

Tennessee

1. Who May Make a Will: Persons of sound mind 18 years of age or older may make a will.
2. Witnesses: Two.
3. Holographic Wills: It is not necessary for a witness to sign a holographic will but the signature and all its material provisions must be in the handwriting of the testator and his handwriting must be proved by two witnesses.
4. Nuncupative Wills: 32-106.

Texas

1. Who May Make a Will: Every person who has attained the age of 18 years, or who is or has been lawfully married, or who is a member of the armed forces of the United States or of the auxiliaries thereof or of the maritime service at the time the will is made, being of sound mind, shall have the right and power to make a last will and testament, under the rules and limitations prescribed by law.
2. Witnesses: Two.
3. Holographic Wills: Where the will is written wholly in the handwriting of the testator, the attesting of the subscribing witnesses may be dispensed with.
4. Nuncupative Wills: Probate Code 64, 65.
5. Revocation: Destroyed or canceled.

Utah

1. Who May Make a Will: Any person 18 years of age or more who is of sound mind may make a will.
2. Witnesses: Two.
3. Holographic Wills: A will which does not comply with Section 75-2-502 is valid as a holographic will, whether or not witnessed, if the signature and the material provisions are in the handwriting of the testator. If there are several holographic wills in existence with conflicting provisions a holographic will to be valid must be dated or circumstances exist that establish which will was last executed.
4. Nuncupative Wills: No provision.
5. Revocation: Burned, torn, canceled, obliterated, or destroyed.

Vermont

1. Who May Make a Will: Every person of full age and sound mind may devise, bequeath, and dispose of his real and personal estate by last will and testament.
2. Witnesses: Three.
3. Holographic Wills: No provision.
4. Nuncupative Wills: 14-6, 7.
5. Revocation: Burned, torn, canceled, or obliterated.

Virginia

1. Who May Make a Will: Any person 18 years of age or

older and of sound mind may make a will.

2. Witnesses: Two.

3. Holographic Wills: If a will be wholly in the handwriting of the testator, neither acknowledgment nor witnesses are necessary. Proof of the handwriting must be by at least two disinterested witnesses.

4. Nuncupative Wills: A soldier in actual service or a mariner or seaman at sea may dispose of personal property by nuncupative will.

5. Revocation: Mutilated or destroyed.

Washington

1. Who May Make a Will: Any person of sound mind who has attained the age of 18 years may make a will.

2. Witnesses: Two.

3. Holographic Wills: No provision.

4. Nuncupative Wills: 11.12.025.

5. Revocation: Burned, torn, canceled, obliterated, or destroyed.

West Virginia

1. Who May Make a Will: Any person except infants and persons of unsound mind, may make a will.

2. Witnesses: Two.

3. Holographic Wills: If a will is wholly in the handwriting of the testator, neither acknowledgment nor witnesses are necessary.

4. Nuncupative Wills: Soldiers in actual military service, and mariners or seamen at sea, may dispose of personal estate as at common law.

5. Revocation: Mutilated, canceled, or destroyed.

Wisconsin

1. Who May Make a Will: Any person of sound mind eighteen years of age or older may make a will.

2. Witnesses: Two.

3. Holographic Wills: No provision.

4. Nuncupative Wills: No provision.

5. Revocation: Burned, torn, canceled, or obliterated.

Wyoming

1. Who May Make a Will: Any adult of sound mind, may dispose by will of all his property except what is sufficient to pay his debts, or what is allowed by law to husband or wife and family.

2. Witnesses: Two.

3. Holographic Wills: An olographic or holographic will as herein defined is one that is entirely written and signed by the hand of the testator himself; and is not required to be in any particular form and may be made in or out of this state, and need not be witnessed.

4. Nuncupative Wills: No provision.

5. Revocation: Burned, torn, canceled, or obliterated.

Glossary of Legal Terms

Abatement

A reduction, a decrease, or a diminution of a legacy under a will.

Acknowledgment

Formal declaration before authorized official, by person who executed instrument, that it is his free act and deed.

Ademption

A person disposing that which he bequeathed under his will so as to make the provision under the will of no effect, that is, selling a watch during his lifetime that he had bequeathed under his will.

Adjusted Gross Estate

Arrived at by deducting estate settlement costs from the gross estate, also known as the taxable estate.

Administration

The management of a decedent's estate.

Administration Expenses

Those necessarily incurred in the administration of the estate, or in the collection of assets, payment of debts, and distribution of property. For example, lawyer fees, executor's fees, appraisal fees, etc.

Administrator

A person appointed by the court to manage and distribute the property of one who dies without a will.

Adultery

Voluntary sexual intercourse of a married person with a person other than the offender's spouse.

Advancement

Money or property given by a parent to a child, which he had previously decided to bequeath under his will and now intends to be deducted from that child's share at the ultimate distribution of the estate under his will.

Ancillary Administration

Administration of a decedent's estate in a state where he had property other than the state he resided in at the time of his death.

Annuity

A yearly payment of money for life or a term of years.

Annulment

Act of annulling; act of making void retrospectively as well as prospectively.

Attestation Clause

The act of witnessing the performance of the statutory requirements as to the valid execution of a will.

Beneficiary

One named in a will to receive a devise or legacy or the use of estate assets.

Bequest

A gift of personal property.

Bigamy

A criminal offense of willfully and knowingly contracting a second marriage while the first marriage, to the knowledge of the offender, is still subsisting and undissolved.

Causa Mortis

In contemplation of approaching death.

Codicil

Addition to or qualification of one's last will.

Common Disaster

The death of two or more persons at the same time and from the same cause, as in the case of an accident.

Common Disaster Clause

A clause under the will which prescribes the order of death as between two or more people who die at the same time.

Common Law

The general and ordinary law of a community receiving its binding force from universal reception. Historically, that body of law and juristic theory which was originated, developed, and formulated in England.

Community Property

The property acquired by either spouse during marriage, other than by gift, devise, or descent based on the doctrine that property acquired during marriage belongs to the marital community. Community property states are Arizona, California, Idaho, Louisiana, Nevada, New Mexico, Texas, and Washington.

Competent Witness

A person who, at the time of attesting to a will, could legally testify in court to the facts to which he attests by subscribing his name to the will.

Conservator

A guardian; protector; preserver.

Corporate Fiduciary

A bank or trust company exercising fiduciary powers under statutory authorization.

Corpus

The principal fund, or capital, upon which income is earned; sometimes called principal.

Credibility

Worthiness of belief; that quality in a witness which renders his evidence worthy of belief.

Curtesy

Under the common law rules a husband had a right in any real property of which his wife was seized at any time during the marriage. The husband's right, termed "curtesy" was inchoate during his wife's lifetime and consummate after her death if he survived her and if a child was born of the marriage. Curtesy entitled the husband to a life estate in all of the wife's freehold property owned by her during the marriage. It could not be defeated by her inter vivos transfer or by the wife's will, and it was not subject to her debts.

Delusion

A belief that something exists which does not exist and which a rational person, in the absence of further proof, would not accept for belief.

Descendent

One who is descended from another; a person who proceeds from the body of another, such as child, grandchild, to the remotest degree.

Descent

Historically the intestate decedent's real property passed

directly to his heirs by operation of law. Thus, real property was said to pass by "descent" to the heirs who took by inheritance.

Descent and Distribution

The distribution of property to heirs and next of kin, as directed by state laws, constituting the estate of a person who dies without a will or leaving an invalid will.

Devise

A gift of real property by will; a "devisor" devises real property to a "devisee" and the disposition is termed a "devise."

Disposing Memory

One in which a person can recall the general nature, condition, and extent of property and his relations to those to whom he gives and to those from whom he withholds that property.

Distribution

Historically this meant title to the intestate decedent's personal property vested in his personal representative who subsequently "distributed" it to the intestate's distributees or next of kin, after the administration of the estate which was the collection and preservation of the decedent's personal property, and the payment of his creditors.

Domicile

That place where a man has his true fixed and permanent home and principal establishment, and to which whenever he is absent he has the intention of returning. It is generally the legal residence of a person which determines the place of probate of a will, the tax situs, and many other legal relationships.

Donee

The person who receives a gift.

Donor

The person making a gift.

Dotage

That feebleness of the mental facilities which proceeds from old age.

Dower

Under the common law rules a wife had a right in any real property of which her husband was seized at any time during the marriage. The wife's right termed "dower," was inchoate during her husband's lifetime and consummate after his death if she survived him. The dower interest was a life estate in one-third of the real property of which the husband had been seized during marriage.

Eccentricity

Personal or individual peculiarities of mind and disposition which markedly distinguish the subject from the ordinary, normal, or average types of men, but do not amount to mental unsoundness or insanity.

Estate

This term refers to all of the property, both real and personal, owned by a decedent at his death and which passes either by his will or by the laws of intestacy. The estate for death tax purposes is not necessarily the same as for administration purposes. The value of many assets may be subject to death taxation though the assets are not subject to administration.

Estate Taxes

Taxes assessed by states and the federal government upon the decedent's right to transfer property.

Exclusion, Annual

The continuing right of a donor to make a tax free gift of up to $3,000 to any number of donees in any year.

Executor (man) or Executrix (woman)

The proper title if the decedent leaves a will designating a personal representative.

Fiduciary

A person holding the character of a trustee, or a character analogous to that of a trustee, in respect to the trust and confidence involved in it and the scrupulous good faith and candor which it requires.

Foreign Will

Will of person not a resident within state at the time of his death.

Fraud

An intentional perversion of truth for the purpose of inducing another, in reliance upon it, to part with some valuable thing belonging to him or to surrender a legal right; a false representation of a matter of fact, whether by words or by conduct, by false or misleading representations, or by concealment of that which should have been disclosed, which deceives, and is intended to deceive another so that he shall act upon it to his legal detriment.

Gift Tax (Federal)

A tax on the donor of inter vivos gifts, based on the right to transfer or transmit, and payable primarily by the donor.

Gross Estate

Includes everything in which the decedent owned an interest at his death, embracing life insurance, joint property, and transfers made in contemplation of death or intended to take effect at or after death, or where the power to change the enjoyment of property has been retained.

Guardian

A person lawfully vested with the power, and charged with the duty, of taking care of a person and managing the property rights of another person, who, for some peculiarity of status, or defect of age, understanding, or self-control, is considered incapable of administering his own affairs.

145

Heirs

Historically this had reference to those who took title to an intestate's real property by descent. Many states now define the word to include those persons who take both real and personal property of the intestate. A living person has no heirs, but only "heirs apparent."

Hallucination

A morbid error in one or more of the senses, or a perception of objects which do not, in fact, make any impression on the external senses. The perception arises not from an impulse received from without, but from a maladjustment within the perceptive apparatus itself. The basic distinction between hallucinations and delusions is that the former refers to false perceptions of objects, while delusions are concerned with false ideas or beliefs.

Holographic Will

A testamentary instrument entirely written, dated, and signed by the testator in his handwriting.

Idiot

A person who has been without understanding from his nativity, and whom the law, therefore, presumes never likely to attain any.

Imminent

Near at hand; close rather than touching; impending; on the point of happening.

Incident of Ownership

Pertaining to ownership of insurance; the retention of an interest by the decedent of more than 5 percent of the policy.

Incidents of Ownership

A term used to describe that amount of control over an asset which would have that asset included as part of one's federal taxable estate.

Incompetency

Lack of ability, legal qualification, or fitness to discharge the required duty.

Inconsistent

Mutually repugnant or contradictory.

In Extremis

An extremity; in the last extremity; in the last illness.

Inheritance Taxes

Taxes assessed on the recipient of the assets and based on the right to receive a decedent's property.

Instrument

A legal document.

Inter Vivos

Between the living; from one living person to another; gifts during one's lifetime.

Intestacy

The state or condition of dying without having made a valid will, or without having disposed by will of a part of his property.

Intestate

Death without a valid will.

Irrevocable

That which cannot be revoked or recalled.

Issue

Children, grandchildren, and others directly descending from a common ancestor.

Joint and Survivor Annuity

An annuity from which one spouse receives the income during his life and upon his death the payments continue for the benefit of the surviving spouse.

Jointly Owned Property

Property owned by two or more persons with the right of ownership in the one or ones who survive; normally unaffected by a will. In certain states, however, it may be willed under well-defined circumstances.

Legatee

One who receives property under a will.

Letters of Administration

Documents issued as proof of authority of an individual to act as administrator.

Letters Testamentary

Documents issued as proof of authority of individual to act as executor.

Life Estate

An interest in property for life.

Litigation

Lawsuit; a contest in a court of justice for the purpose of enforcing a right.

Lunatic

A person of deranged or unsound mind; a person whose mental facilities are in the condition called "lunacy," one who possessed reason, but through disease, grief, or other cause, has lost it.

Lucid Interval

A temporary cure; a temporary restoration to sanity.

Marital Deduction

A deduction for federal estate tax purposes from the gross estate of property passing to a surviving spouse in a manner conforming to the law; the deduction is limited to 50 percent of the adjusted gross estate or $250,000, whichever amount is greater.

Monomania

In medical jurisprudence, derangement of a single facility of the mind, or with regard to a particular subject, the other facilities being in regular exercise.

Non Compos Mentis

A condition approximating total and positive incompetency. It denotes a person entirely destitute of memory and understanding.

Nuncupative Will

An oral declaration by a testator in extremis, or under circumstances considered equivalent thereto, as to the final disposition of his property, made before witnesses, and subsequently reduced to writing by someone other than the testator. Specific requirements and limitations are set out in the statutes in the states where these wills are valid.

Obliteration

Erasure or blotting out of written words.

Paranoia

Delusional insanity or monomania.

Partial Insanity

A term applied to cases wherein the mind is clouded or weakened, but is not entirely incapable of remembering, reasoning, or judging.

Perjury

The willful assertion as to a matter of fact, opinion, belief, or knowledge, made by a witness in a judicial proceeding as part of his evidence, either upon oath or in any form allowed by law to be substituted for an oath, whether such evidence is given in open court, or in an affidavit, or otherwise, such assertion being material to the issue or point of inquiry and known to such witness to be false.

Per Capita

Equally, or share and share alike.

Per Stirpes

According to the roots, or by right of representation; the issue of deceased children will take their deceased parent's share by right of representation; that mode of reckoning the rights or liabilities of descendants in which the children or any one descendant has to take only the share which their parents would have taken, if alive. For example, suppose a decedent had three children, Jim, Jane, and John, who, if living, would get one-third each. If John predeceased the decedent and left ten children, the estate would be divided into twelve equal shares, if per capita. If per stirpes, the estate would be one-third to Jane, one-third to Jim, and the remaining one-third divided among John's ten children.

Probate

This word describes the presenting of the will to the appropriate court to establish its validity, and the entering of the court's order finding that the instrument is decedent's will and admitting it to "probate." There follows, as in intestate estates, a process of "administration," the collection, and preservation of a decedent's property to those entitled to it by his will or by the statute of descent and distribution.

Publication

The communication by the testator to the witnesses of his intention that the instrument in question should take effect as his will.

Realty

A brief term for real property; also everything which partakes of the nature of real property.

Residuary Clause

All that is left after indebtedness and bequests, or gifts, are paid.

Residuary Estate

All that is left of a testator's estate after all liabilities are discharged and all his bequests and devises are paid.

Revocation of Will

The recalling, annulling, or rendering inoperative of an existing will, by some subsequent act of the testator, which may be by the making of a new will inconsistent with the term of the first, or by destroying the old will, or by disposing of the property to which it related, or otherwise.

Spendthrift

One who spends money in an unwise manner; one who wastes his estate.

Spendthrift Trust

A trust created to provide a fund for the maintenance of a beneficiary, and at the same time protect this fund against the beneficiary's incapacity or improvidence and also against claims of creditors.

Spouse's Right of Election

A spouse's right to elect a statutory share of the deceased spouse's estate in lieu of what was left under the will.

Statute

An act of the legislature declaring, commanding, or prohibiting something, a particular law enacted and established by the will of the legislature; the written will of the legislature, solemnly expressed according to the forms necessary to constitute it the law of the state.

Statutory Share

That portion of a person's property allowed to the spouse by statute.

Subscribe

To write your name yourself; literally to write underneath or to write below a documentary statement and in its popular meaning is usually limited to a signature at the end of a printed or written instrument.

Subscribing Witnesses

Those who sign as witnesses to a will.

Temporary Insanity

A temporary derangement which may result from any transient condition, as, for example, intoxication.

Testamentary

The expression of an intent to dispose of property in a will.

Testamentary Capacity

The competency to make a will.

Testamentary Power

A person who may make a will.

Testate

Death leaving a valid will.

Testator

One who dies leaving a will.

Testimonium Clause

The execution of a will; that clause of a will or instrument which concludes, "IN WITNESS WHEREOF, I . . ."

Trust

In general, a right of property, real or personal, held by one party for the benefit of another.

Trustee

A person holding the trust property for the benefit of others.

Unreasonable

Irrational, foolish, unwise, absurd, silly, preposterous, senseless, stupid, not reasonable, immoderate.

Valid

Sufficiently supported by actual fact, well grounded, sound, or just, good or effective, having sufficient legal strength or force, good or sufficient in point of law.

Validity

The state or quality of being valid, legal strength or force, soundness.

Void

Having no legal or binding force, null. Empty or not containing matter, vacant, unoccupied, devoid, destitute.

Will

An instrument executed by a competent person in the manner prescribed by statute, whereby he makes a disposition of his property to take effect on and after his death.

Willful

Proceeding from a conscious motive of the will; voluntary.

Witness

One who, being present, personally sees or perceives a thing, a beholder, spectator, or eyewitness. One who testifies to what he has seen, heard, or otherwise observed or learned.

A FREE ISSUE OF THE *CITIZEN'S LAW ADVISOR* IS WAITING FOR YOU!

Dear Friend,

Although this is the end of the book, it's just the beginning for you!

The *CITIZEN'S LAW ADVISOR* is a quarterly newspaper packed with human interest stories, advice on how readers are using the *CITIZEN'S LAW LIBRARY,* insights into tax shelters and other income sheltering and producing items, plus a complete book review and bookshelf section listing other titles in the field of layperson's law published by Prentice-Hall, Inc.

To receive your free complimentary issue of the *CITIZEN'S LAW ADVISOR* simply write your name and address on the coupon below and mail the coupon without further delay. Or call, toll-free, 1-800-228-2054 and tell the operator where you saw this announcement.

I look forward to hearing from you!

Sincerely yours,

J. Stephen Lanning

J. Stephen Lanning
Executive Vice President
Citizen's Law Library

CITIZENS LAW LIBRARY, Box 1745, 7 South Wirt Street, Leesburg, Va. 22075

Yes, please send me a free complimentary copy of the latest issue of THE CITIZENS LAW ADVISOR.

Signature _____

Name _____

Address _____

City _____ State _____ Zip _____

EPFSBO